MW01290161

Mary Kathleen

The Unseen Voice

Copyright © 2019 Mary Kathleeen ISBN:
Scripture quotations taken from The Holy Bible, *New International Version*®, *NIV*®. Copyright © 1973, 1978, 1984 by Biblica, Inc. ™ Used by permission of Zondervan. All rights reserved worldwide.

All Rights Reserved. No part of this publication may be reproduced, stored in a retrieval system, or transmitted in any form or by any means – electronic, mechanical, photocopy, recording, or any other – except for brief quotations in printed reviews, without the prior permission of the author.

ISBN: 9781097767922

Printed in the United States of America

FOREWORD

The Unseen Voice is the story of a child raised without the love, acceptance and support so vital for survival. Neglected and ignored, she felt invisible.

In spite of her loveless environment, God had plans for Mary. Miraculously, God spoke to her as The Unseen Voice at an early age. She recognized His voice and remembered what He said.

She built her life around His words, graduated from high school a Straight-A Student and moved out of her parent's house. She married her high school sweetheart, a wonderful man she chose at 16 because she knew he would be a good husband.

She came to the Lord by herself. He sat her down with His Word and taught her singlehandedly. God prepared her for the journey He designed for her. Her life has never been free of pain and challenges, but God has used them all to make her the Warrior she is today. Every word of this story is true.

Faith Allen

Contents

Foreword   iii

Welcome To A Broken World   1

Going Home   8

Character And Traits   17

Strength And Wisdom   27

Two Become One   44

The Unseen Power   52

Filling Empty Spaces   68

Transplanted And Pruned   77

Ministry In Mo-Town   90

Armies They Know Not Of   104

Epilogue   117

Welcome to a Broken World

On a cold day in February, 1950, baby Mary was born. A nurse pushed on top of her mother while a doctor pulled on her head. Her mother slept soundly so she would feel no pain.

Mary was smaller than normal because Carol smoked during her pregnancy. When she entered the world, Mary was given oxygen-- good for the brain, bad for the eyesight. Little farsighted Mary cried. There would be many more tears.

If the curtain could have been pulled back to expose the unseen world, the nurse and doctor would have seen a tremendous battle launching for the life and soul of this insignificant baby. Unwanted, unkept, rejected, and excluded from her family, God's mark on Mary was distinctive and would never come off.

The Unseen Voice gave her name to her parents, Mary (woman of many sorrows and carrier of Christ) Kathleen (pure and virginal) and set about to use her giftings in a broken world. His ways are not rushed. There was time to mold this precious baby girl. She had more fortitude than anyone would ever realize, including herself. That determination fit in perfectly for the plans He had designed.

The other voice had plans to stop her. This underweight farsighted baby girl was a huge threat. Satan did not know why, but he knew it. Mary's life was forever connected to the eternal spiritual realm.

Carol and Jim wanted a boy, Jim, Jr., named after his father. They already had a two-year-old daughter, Priscilla. On the next try, they got the boy they wanted. They were done with having babies. She was an invisible child in a broken world.

Priscilla had the upper hand and knew how to keep Mary out of the sight of her parents. She knew how to hurt Mary. Jim, Jr. was her dad's pride and joy, spoiled and given things he did not need which did not satisfy. Having a son did not keep Jim home. Between tennis, bowling leagues and going to Mason's meetings with his friends, he was of little help for Mary's mom, Carol.

At four years old, Mary woke up and started to cry. This cry had been in her gut for a long time, and finally broke loose. She sounded as if someone had smacked her. It woke everyone in the house. Her parents came running and asked her what was wrong.

The words tumbled out, "Nobody loves me!"

"That's ridiculous," Carol said. They turned around and went back to bed.

That morning was the first time Mary heard The Unseen Voice. Still sniffling from the cry, it was clear as a bell. A man's voice said, *"Don't let them define who you are!"*

Mary had no idea what the word "define" meant. Someday she would know what it was. She quit crying and went back to being the invisible child. But she tried not to be so sad about it.

The second voice came a couple years later when Mary stood in front of her dresser admiring the quarters she was saving to buy a horse. That voice said, *"Worship money"*.

Mary jumped because it frightened her. There must be two different voices. She decided to never worship money, whatever that meant. She ran out of her room, terrified and wondered what worshipping money involved.

One night her family went out for dinner. Traffic came to a crawl, down to one lane. As they slowly passed the lane that was closed, Mary saw the problem. A beautiful Collie dog had been hit by a car. Blood pooled around her head turning the cement red. The dog's eyes were open, but empty.

The owner and the driver were screaming at each other. Mary guessed they both did something wrong. But her family just drove on like nothing happened. They had a good dinner, and never discussed it.

Mary could not eat anything and did not sleep for three nights. Every time she closed her eyes, she saw the poor Collie's empty eyes and the pool of blood. Mary's first experience with death left a pit in her stomach. She decided she did not fit in with her family, and this world was not a good place to live. Something was terribly wrong.

Mary spent a few summers with her grandparents in Iowa. Jim, Jr. and Priscilla stayed home. Iowa was hot, humid, and smelled musty, but had beautiful big trees.

At her grandparent's house Mary was cared for and loved. Although they never said it, Mary knew by the way they looked at her. They saw her. She was happy there.

Grandma bathed her and combed her hair. She touched Mary and sometimes held her small hand. Grandma sat with her on the back steps. They took pits out of cherries, just the right amount for one cherry pie.

On the weekends, Grandpa walked Mary into town to the swimming pool. He stood outside the fence and never took his eyes off of her. Mary did not know how to swim, but the water was cool, and she could see her grandpa watching. That made her feel safe.

While Mary was at her grandparent's house, she learned a lot. Sliding down the bannister was fun. Sleeping in a feather bed felt like you were being cuddled. Right after a bath, it was the best feeling ever to run and jump in the bed. The tin roof sounded like bullets when it rained. The lightning would hit the street and spread out like a yellow spider.

Grandma and Grandpa had a basement you had to get to from outside the house. It was cool and damp dark with dirt floors and had shelves of canned fruit and vegetables all around.

An old wringer washing machine stood in the center of the floor, right under one little light hanging down from the ceiling on a black cord. Although Mary could not touch the dangerous wringer, she liked to sit on the steps and watch Grandma wind the handle.

Mary wanted to go to the basement by herself to get a little cooler. On one of the steps was a dead bird with little feet sticking straight up. Mary backed out and did not go back to the basement for a long time. She hated dead things of the world.

Bats flew around at night, trying to eat bugs. One night a bat flew all over the ceiling. Mary had never seen a bat, but the noise and shadow were familiar. Many times, as she laid in her bed at home, she would see the shadows and hear the movement. She would put her head under her pillow and wait for it to stop.

The Unseen Voice would say, "Be strong, Mary, be strong!"

At Grandma's house, Mary met some interesting people. One day she was sitting on the living room floor playing cards when the doorbell rang. Grandma ran from the kitchen and started picking up every card Mary had on the floor. She put the cards in a drawer, straightened her apron, and opened the door.

It was a church lady who wanted to discuss sin with Grandma. Mary wanted to hear this and since they did not ask her to leave, she was good at being invisible.

The church lady talked long and loud about mothers who worked being the worst kind of sinners. Their kids would grow up to be God-haters and criminals. Maybe even smoke or drink! Mary was all ears because her mother worked and she had never heard of such a thing.

Next, Mary found out that not only having mothers working was a sin, but playing cards, going to movies, wearing open-toed shoes, cursing, and not going to church at least twice a week were all very big sins. People who passed by the Salvation Army bucket without putting a nickel in were big sinners. Clothes needed to cover all of your body and not be tight so people could guess what you looked like naked. You could make men sin in their heads just by looking at you.

Mary tugged at her shorts to try to make them look longer. She decided she would try to stay away from men, except her grandpa. Wearing lipstick, eyeshadow or red nail polish was also a sin. Hair had to be long and combed.

If Jesus came back to take His beloved children to heaven and you were in a movie theater, you would not get to go. You would have to stay on earth and be tribulated, whatever that meant. Mary had only been to a movie twice, but decided next time she would hurry out of the theater as soon as the movie was over and not wait for the credits to end and the lights to come on--just in case. Mary's grandma did not say much, but listened and nodded her head once in a while. Maybe Grandma could not hear what the church lady was saying because she had Scarlet Fever as a child and lost most of her hearing.

Mary did not agree about the working mothers. If her mother did not work, she would lie in bed for weeks depressed and would maybe kill herself, because her dad told her, "You girls be good or Mother is going to kill herself!" This depressed Mary.

Mary knew better than to ask a question. It might be a sin for a little girl to talk to grownups while they are talking, especially about something as important as sin.

Mary did not know if playing cards was a sin. But Grandma must think it was okay as long as you put the cards away before you answered the door. After that day, when Mary played cards, she sat close to the table with the drawer ready at all times to pick them up in a hurry and put them in.

Once a week Grandpa gave Mary a quarter and took her to Woolworth 5&10 store in town. Mary walked up and down every aisle and looked at everything.

Grandpa was patient and stood watching over her. He was not in a hurry. Mary would pick something up, turn it over and put it back. This lasted a long time. Mary never bought anything for herself. She bought some Evening in Paris perfume for her mom, a necklace for her sister, a comic book for her brother, and a handkerchief for her dad in case he got a runny nose.

It took her a while to save up enough money for all her purchases. She finally had a few quarters left over to put with her other quarters at home for her horse. This was her dream from as far back as she could remember.

For one week every summer everybody from Iowa who belonged to Grandpa's kind of church went to revival campout. Mary did not know why they needed to be revived. They looked okay to her.

Grandpa set up a tent and gave Mary a coffee can in case she had to go to the bathroom in the middle of the night. Sleeping on the ground was not like the soft featherbed at Grandma's. Mary was worried she might move wrong and knock the can over. Beetles shrieked loud noises all night.

Revival was fun, although the church lady was there making her way through the camp and talking to people about sin, Mary always tried to be going the other way.

They had a lot of activities for the kids during the day. One afternoon they all made Plaster of Paris Ten Commandments. Mary's came out exceptionally good, and she was proud of it. She wanted to take it home and put it on her dresser next to her quarters for her horse.

Mary could think of one more commandment God could have told Moses to write, "Love ALL your children," but she didn't say anything. Every time she touched her Ten Commandments, she felt a tingle go through her because this was God's Word. She loved them, especially since they had nothing to say about wearing shorts, open-toed shoes and working mothers.

One afternoon all the children went to the Lake to cool off. They piled in old pickup trucks and men drove them to the lake. All the kids were excited except Mary. She looked every man over driving a truck and thought some were alright and some were not. She did not know why, but she picked one who looked alright to ride with.

She went to the edge of the Lake and looked in and it was murky and muddy. As the other kids played for two hours and had lots of fun, Mary stood at the edge of the lake watching her toes so nothing could creep up on her.

At night they made bonfires that lit up a whole stack of wood to roast marshmallows. Grandpa roasted the marshmallows because he did not want Mary to fall in the fire and burn up.

It was finally time to pack up and head home. As they slowly drove back, Mary looked carefully at her grandma and grandpa to see if they had been revived. She could not tell any difference, but maybe it was something you could not see.

She held her prized Ten Commandments all the way home, because she did not want it to get broken in the trunk with all the camping equipment. She did not understand all the commandments, but she knew there was something important about them.

In Grandma's living room was a big piano. Mary suspected this was the piano her mom played and took lessons on to become the best pianist in all of Iowa. She would travel to competitions and always won. Mary had seen the cut-out newspaper articles with pictures of her mother wearing beautiful long lace gowns and big bouquets of flowers for winning first prize.

She was told by many people that someday she would play in Carnegie Hall and be rich and famous in New York City. She was the "Pride of Iowa."

Maybe that was why Carol was so depressed all the time. Instead of being rich and famous living in New York City, she was in a little house in Denver with three young kids fighting.

Mary's dad, Jim, was first-chair clarinet, and sometimes traveled with Big Bands from back east who needed an extra clarinetist when they performed in Iowa. He was that good!

Carol met Jim, in high school band. Jim was a senior, Carol was a freshman. Jim started riding his bike up and down and up and down Carol's street and Carol would wave to him out the window. Grandpa was not happy about that one bit! Grandpa thought Jim was too old for his youngest daughter. Soon they were dating.

GOING HOME

Mary had been waiting all summer for her family to come get her. In her imagination, she pictured a grand welcome as if they had missed her as much as she missed them. The day they finally arrived, her family was tired of riding in the car, and walked right by her without a word. She went upstairs and cried for a while, then came down with their gifts.

Mary's suffering was about to begin again, back with her family where she was invisible. But her suffering created in her a great wisdom she would not have had without it.

Mary's world was one of unfulfilled expectations. She would have high hopes about the way things should be, but they would never turn out that way. Disappointment led to depression. She was always being told by the evil voice that something was terribly wrong with her.

But The Unseen Voice would say, "Be strong, Mary, be strong." The battle for Mary never stopped.

Her family did not think much of their gifts because they were cheap. When Carol was not looking, Mary took the Evening in Paris perfume back for herself. Her mother never missed it.

Jim took a long nap. After a big dinner, they traveled home at night because it was a little cooler and the kids would sleep and not fuss. Mary was too excited about going home to sleep.

Blinking red lights lit up the road. Mary knew there was a problem, and her dad slowed down. Highways were only two-lane roads and they seemed to go up and down like roller coasters.

Mary strained and saw a dead horse lying in the road. Blood was all over. About eight policemen were standing around talking about what to do and scratching their heads. This sight was the third dead animal Mary had seen. As much as she loved horses, this hit the hardest.

Why do animals and people have to die?

Jim slowed down, but kept on going. Soon, he was pulled over. Blinking red lit up the whole inside of the car.

The officer wrote Jim a ticket for not coming to a complete stop back at the accident.

Carol leaned over from the passenger side and yelled at the policeman in a voice Mary was familiar with, "We do not have any money to pay your damn ticket, so if you want to put two adults and three children in your jail, you go right ahead!" He closed his book, turned around and went back to the dead horse.

Jim started driving again. As soon as he could no longer see the red lights behind him, he sped up. He was a fast driver and the speedometer would often hit 100 mph. That is as high as it would go. He laughed at the way Carol handled the situation. If you were "The Pride of Iowa," you could do as you pleased.

Mary knew what awaited her. Nobody in the house would talk to her, look at her, or be friendly. She had heard the opposite of love was hate, but she knew the opposite of love was being ignored.

They finally made it home early in the morning. Mary was tired. The first thing she did was put her three quarters, Evening in Paris perfume and her plaster of Paris Ten Commandments on her dresser. Before she fell asleep, she spoke to The Unseen Voice. "Thank you for watching out for us, for keeping us out of jail, and especially for giving me the love I felt from my grandma and grandpa. Even though I was homesick, I felt their love."

Jim was as good at tennis as he was playing the clarinet. At one time he was ranked in the top 100. When he would go play tennis at City Park in Denver, Carol would tell him to take Mary. He might play tennis for five hours. Mary often walked to the Museum of Natural History on the other side of the park by herself. She would hide in a dark room that wasn't locked where butterflies and beetles were pinned to cardboard for displays. She also would look at the big dinosaur all put together who could eat a little girl with one bite.

When she got back to the tennis courts, she waited until her dad was finished. He always won. He had not looked for her or noticed she had been gone for hours. He was concentrating on winning tennis, not watching out for his little blond daughter.

They would go to San Diego to see their friends, and all the way to San Francisco where Mary's other grandpa lived. He was not as interested in his grandchildren as Mary's grandparents from Iowa. His wife died of cancer at 50. The last time Mary saw her in San Francisco, she was near death, screaming and moaning for morphine. They were terrible sounds Mary never forgot.

These grandparents once lived in Denver, but were not interested in seeing their grandkids. One day, Carol took the kids shopping. The girls had to go to the bathroom so she stopped at her mother-in-law's house. Grandma Irene told Carol she could not let her kids in to use the bathroom because she had just finished washing the floors. She would never smile or speak to her grandkids, Carol or her son. They were all invisible.

Mary learned her dad's grandmother was a psychic who read tarot cards and people's futures and fortunes by tea leaves for money. Mary had a bad feeling about that whole side of the family and she did not want to be around them. Sometimes her dad would make her spend the night with his grandma and Mary could not wait to get out of there.

She saw people who came over to have their futures read. Mary could hear talking coming from somewhere. It sounded like her plastic radio trying to find a station, but Mary knew it was not something from this world. Something was telling her great grandmother what to say. Someone else in her family inherited this power and if she got mad at someone and wanted them hurt, the next thing you know, they broke a leg.

Mary was afraid. The Unseen Voice would say, "Be strong, Mary, be strong." She tried, but she was only a little girl.

If they took a vacation going west, Carol always wanted to stop in Las Vegas to gamble and drink. The casinos were strict about letting kids inside, so the three kids stood outside in the heat and cried as they looked in the window. They watched their mom put quarters in the slot machines. Mary hoped she would lose all those quarters in a hurry.

Sometimes they tried to get close to the doors where air-conditioned coolness would hit their faces. Jim did not like to gamble, drink or smoke, so he sat down next to Carol and watched her.

Mary knew this might be another sin the church lady had not thought about being so far from Iowa.

On Sunday mornings, Mary was drawn to go to church. She would get up early, put on her best clothes and walk around the corner to a little white church. She would stand there until the people started coming and wait for somebody to open the heavy door so she could walk in with them. She went downstairs to find a class with kids her age. She would sit in and listen. Nobody knew she was gone from home, and nobody at the church knew she did not belong to one of their families.

She heard Bible stories from an easy-to-understand point of view. She would leave as soon as Sunday School was over and before the Church service started upstairs, run home, put her pajamas back on and get back into bed. Everybody slept in on Sundays so Mary knew no one would hear her leave or come home.

Mary's biggest fear was that her mom would die in a car accident on her way home from work. From 4:30 to 6:30, Mary would turn on a local radio station (KIMN) on her little plastic radio and listen to the traffic reports between the hit songs. Carol had to drive through the Mouse Trap where two major highways crossed and the roads were going every which way. Accidents always happened there.

Because a helicopter flew overhead, the traffic guy would give the color of the cars in the accidents. Mary would almost hold her breath until her mom walked in the door. She knew her dad could not raise his kids. What would happen if her mother died? Mary also worried about her mother's drinking, smoking, taking pills and the depression which could cause her to commit suicide. She got pills from different doctors and had the prescriptions delivered from different pharmacies. She worried about too many things.

Mary's favorite place to be was school and she was excited to start second grade. She was ready to speak up and ask questions. In kindergarten the teacher sent a note home pinned to Mary's blouse. It said, "Mary needs her eyes checked."

Mary got the glasses she needed, but not without her parents complaining about the cost. Her glasses would become her Christmas present. Christmas was not a happy time as she watched Priscilla and Jim Jr. get the gifts they wanted.

One Christmas her parents wrapped up a watch with Mary's name on it. Mary listened to it and heard it tick. She was so excited. But on Christmas morning, the watch went to Priscilla. They only put Mary's name on it so Priscilla would not open it early.

The first thing Mary did every morning, was put on her glasses so she could see. She never forgot them.

In school, Mary asked questions like "What does 'define' mean?" (She never forgot the word The Unseen Voice told her.) "If someone kills a dog with their car, is that sin considered murder?"

"Do people get buried naked?" "If your grandma gets her hair done and it comes out blue, should you tell her?" "What is adultery?"

After that question the teacher asked Mary to come up to her desk and ask her questions without the whole class hearing. Mary finally found out what all the Ten Commandments meant. She was not sure she was doing all of them, because she wanted something somebody else had--a family she was not invisible in.

She had a question the teacher had no answer for, "When I see out of my eyes, and you see out of your eyes, is everything the same or do we see things different and we do not know it?"

Gym class was twice a week, and Mary was supposed to bring gym shorts for the class. The problem was, Carol never had them washed and ready. Mary, humiliated, had to do gym in her dress. If she climbed the ropes or swung on the monkey bars, the boys would stand below looking up her dress laughing. The ropes she had to climb up would put big red marks on her legs.

Mary had holes in her socks. She wore hand-me-down shoes from her sister that were too tight. Mary learned to pull the holes in the heels below the shoe line so they could not be seen. This made Mary nervous, looking at the back of her shoes all day to see if the holes were still hidden.

Mary's arms were always dirty because after dinner she would take a spoon from the kitchen drawer to dig a hole to China under the swing-set. Mary did not know what China would be like, but she heard they were starving and she wanted to take them a box of rice. Carol did not bathe Mary like her grandma did. She never looked at Mary or noticed her dirty arms, feet, and holes in her socks.

One day Mary's teacher said, "Mary, your arms are very dirty." Mary said, "If you think my arms are dirty, you should see my feet!"

The teacher walked off laughing. Mary tried to keep her arms under her desk, but it was hard when she had to write something. No one in school invited her over for a play date, probably because she was so unclean.

Mary was left-handed. They strapped a metal contraption on her right hand with a pencil in it to change her to right-handed. Mary thought this made her look more of a dork with glasses and dirty arms and all. She did learn to write right-handed although she never understood why she could not be what she was.

Mary shared a table with Roxanne, but they did not speak. Roxanne had the whitest arms Mary had ever seen. They sparkled. Also, her hair was not all over the place like Mary's. Nobody got Mary ready for school like Carol did Priscilla. Roxanne's hair was a beautiful reddish blond in neat pig-tails or braids with a different colored ribbon every day.

Mary decided if she ever had a little girl, she would learn how to do pig-tails and braids and save her money for a lot of different colored ribbons so her daughter could look like Roxanne. She would keep her gym shorts ready, get her new socks when they started wearing thin in the heels, and new underwear with no holes in them either. Mary wrote all this down so she would not ever forget.

The absolute worst thing were those darned Russian bomb drills. The bell would ring, then the principal would come over a loud speaker to say it was a bomb drill, otherwise you might think it was a fire drill and start running out of the building and get hit on the head with a bomb. Everyone had to stop, go out of the classroom into the hall, sit under coat racks, put their heads between their knees and wait. Either a bomb would hit you or a bell would ring again.

Mary hated the Russian bomb drills! She moved slowly and tried to be the last one out of the room. She looked across the hall to find a bunch of girls sitting together from another class. She scooted in across from them so no boys could see her underpants. Mary could not figure out how in the world your knees would save your head from a nuclear bomb all the way from Russia. She hated those Russians for making her do this. They wanted to hit her head with a bomb, and what did she ever do to them? She did not even know them. How stupid was that!

Mary was quite a tomboy. She always hung out with the boys who lived across the street, Kevin and Tommy, and could beat them up until she couldn't. It was not a mean fight, but a strength fight to see who was the strongest. After the fight they all laughed and rode their bikes together.

She was the fastest girl in her school, could beat everyone at tetherball and four-square, hit a baseball farther than the boys. Boys picked her first for their team.

Deep down, Mary wished she was a boy because she might have been treated better and she wanted to learn how to play tennis. Mary's dad did not think tennis was for girls. Chrissie Everet had not started winning championships yet. When she did, it was too late for Mary to be any good at it.

When Mary started third grade, the school realized how smart she was. They put her in a class with half of the smartest third graders and half fourth graders. Mary loved it!

Mary started throwing up every night. She had a "nervous stomach." No one knew it because she did it in the washtub in the basement. She cleaned the sink with Comet then went back to bed.

During her yearly physical, the doctor was concerned because Mary lost weight from the year before. She was taller and should have been gaining. He did blood tests, but did not find anything. Nothing was done about it. Mary was always hungry, but could not keep the food down. She worried about everything. At school lunch, Mary would ask everyone around her if they were going to eat their spinach. She ate what nobody else wanted. She also ate baked potato skins before they were popular when she did the dishes at home. She would salt and pepper them and set them aside.

When Mary was eight, Jim went into Jim Jr.'s bedroom to wake him up for dinner. He was not breathing and turning black. Jim called the para-medics who came right away and pronounced him dead.

Carol screamed, Jim cried, and the para-medics ran in and out of the house. Mary felt as if her life was over.

Then a man walked into the house and said to Mary and Priscilla, "Go across the street and stay with your neighbors. Your brother will be fine." They did.

At some point, Jim, Jr. started breathing again. He was in a coma for a long time. The doctors told Carol and Jim to pray he would die because his brain would be damaged and would be a vegetable. Mary thought that was strange.

One day, he woke up normal as could be. They discovered measles had broken out in his brain causing it to swell and he had encephalitis. Mary and Priscilla believed everybody heard the man who walked into their living room. They found out later only they heard him. They believed what he said because he spoke as one who had authority.

Mary's Uncle Melvin asked her, "Did this man look like the Jesus you see in pictures?"

"No. He had on a beige shirt, khaki slacks, a belt, and socks and shoes. No beard. He looked like an average man."

Uncle Melvin said, "That's right! Anybody who says they have seen Jesus says He looks nothing like the picture of Him."

Mary did not know if she had seen Jesus or not. It could be no one else was paying attention. But one thing was for sure—the man was the only one who believed Jim, Jr. would be fine.

All of Mary's relatives came to Denver for a visit.

They all went out to dinner for Chinese food. When the desert came, it was a little bowl of vanilla ice cream. Grandpa didn't want his. All the grandkids were clamoring for it. He picked up his ice cream bowl and sat it down in front of Mary.

He would never know what that meant to her. "*I am his favorite,*" she thought and slowly ate the ice cream in case anyone else wanted another look.

Mary loved her Uncle Jack, Aunt Doris and her cousins. One night, a tornado demolished their home but they were safe in a tornado shelter. It was the one and only time they went to a tornado shelter. It was a miracle. The next day, Mennonites came to help them clean up. Later they built a modern house with a basement that had their own shelter.

When Mary was much older, she was a Railroad Chaplain of America. She drove through Kansas night or day when families lost a loved one in a train accident. She met people on the worst day of their lives. On her way back to Kansas City, Mary always drove by her aunt and uncle's farm because she loved them so much. They were so good to her even when she was invisible.

Mary's grandparents, aunts, uncles and cousins lived a long way from Denver. They were instrumental in giving Mary a glimmer of hope. They helped her believe she had something good in her because they loved her.

When she was a Chaplain, both her aunts and uncles asked Mary to pray for them the last time she saw them alive. It felt as if they were passing the torch to the next generation. Mary felt happy they chose her to carry on their faith and goodness. She would try.

CHARACTER AND TRAITS

Before fifth grade, Mary's family moved to a different area. This house was a new build and bigger, but the sisters still had to share a bedroom.

One day at Montgomery Wards, Mary signed up for a contest to win a private telephone. She won! The telephone people came and installed a pink princess phone in her bedroom with her own number and her name in the white pages of the telephone book. They never turned it off.

Priscilla cried, but Mary would not let her use her phone. Nobody could listen in on Mary's phone conversations like they did at Grandma's house on the party line.

Mary decided the best way to get out of this family was to look for someone who would make a good husband, get married and have a family where she was not invisible. To do that, she wanted to study character and traits of boys to understand what would make a good husband and what would not. She got a spiral notebook to write this information down as she was going to study this subject like she would study anything else. Mary loved to study.

Valentine's Day fell on a Saturday. Three boys came to her house at different times with Valentine gifts for Mary. Two of them had boxes of chocolates which Mary loved. Joe had a pair of white gloves he made out of rabbit fur he shot hunting with his dad. Mary felt sorry for the rabbit, but loved the gloves. No one came with a gift for Priscilla.

Mary's parents yelled at her and called her boy-crazy. They said she would be pregnant by the time she was 13. Mary wrote in her spiral notebook, "Do not get pregnant at 13." She added, "Do not let them define who you are," and "Do not worship money." These things seemed important and she needed to keep them in her notebook. She was well aware her life was connected to an eternal spiritual realm, but she did not understand it.

She did not try to explain to her parents that she was studying boys to find out good characteristics and traits to find a good husband, one who loved her. She did not think they would believe, care or understand. They were busy working with her sister and brother to make them great.

Behind the curtain the devil said, "Mary is going to be destroyed. She is not strong enough to endure this." The Unseen Voice said, "She is going to get stronger even if she has to suffer alone."

Mary figured her mother and father were going to make sure Mary's sister and brother lived out their unfulfilled dreams. There was no dream of theirs left over for Mary, so she had to come up with one of her own.

In the fifth grade Mary started playing the flute and she was very good at it. In fact, she was so good that she had a solo part in about every concert. Mary had perfect pitch. No one in her family ever came to any of Mary's concerts except one. Mary's mom was to accompany her on the piano for Ave Maria. All week long, Mary's mom yelled at her to practice. She did not think Mary could play such a difficult piece in her first year of learning the flute, especially in front of so many people. Mary would not practice.

She said, "I only have to play it right once. No need practicing."

Carol was afraid Mary would embarrass her. The night of the concert, Mary played Ave Maria beautifully. Her tone was flawless. Her mother, however, "The Pride of Iowa," flubbed up. Go figure.

Mary thought if she was good at music, her parents might like her. They did not. In fact, they skipped parent/teacher conferences, back-to-school nights or anything else that had to do with Mary.

She rode her bicycle up to the Drug Store with a soda fountain, bought a lime Coke with her babysitting money and looked through any magazine that might have an article about marriage.

As Mary read, "Can this marriage be saved?" She wrote down what could make it saved and what would make it not able to be saved. She talked on her pink phone with boys in her class, wrote down their names and what their character was like--things she liked about them and things she did not.

She decided one of the best characteristics was a good heart, caring about other people, not just yourself. Being smart was important. This eliminated a lot of boys at that age. If all they did was talk about themselves, she crossed them off. She wanted to find someone like her Uncle Jack because she admired his honesty and caring. It was hard to figure out if a boy was honest.

One boy she knew was not honest because he stole money from the teacher's desk. She wrote him off. Mary figured, she did not have to find the boy now who would be her husband, just the good traits and bad traits to look for when she was ready for a husband. There might be more to choose from later. That took the pressure off. She had time.

Sixth grade came, Mary's last year in grade school. One day she got sick at school and needed to go home. She was sent to the Principal's office. The Principal told Mary to call her mom to come pick her up. Mary knew right away that would not work. Her mother would never leave work across town to come and take her home. She did not know what to do. She started dialing random numbers and accidentally dialed her best friend's number. Vicki's mother answered and thought it was Vicki. She said she would be right there. Mary thought it would be wonderful to have a mother like that.

Mary made a bee-line for the school parking lot and walked home sick before Vicki's mother got there. Mary apologized to Vicki, but not the Principal.

The gym teacher told the class only problem students were put in Mr. Hulse's sixth-grade class. Mary knew she was not the problem, her mother was. Her mom would be drinking late at night and call the teacher or Principal if she thought they had done something wrong. It was embarrassing and made Mary afraid to go to school. But nobody ever called her out of class. They just put her in Mr. Hulse's class with all the problem children.

Nevertheless, Mary hit the jackpot with Mr. Hulse as her teacher. He was a good male-figure in her life. He knew what he was doing and taught Mary well. He let the students give a 10-minute speech on anything they wanted right after lunch for extra credit. Mary always had one she was working on.

For example, the esophagus. She asked a boy in the class to stand on his head and eat a piece of bread to show it did not work by gravity. Food would go up in the esophagus. Everyone thought it was funny. Giving those short speeches helped Mary not be afraid to stand up and talk in front of people. Public speaking was something good to be able to do.

Mr. Hulse walked around the room and bonked Mary on the head with a yardstick because she was talking to everybody around her. He only had to do it once! After that, Mary looked straight ahead.

Believe it or not, Mary thought that was a good trait Mr. Hulse would not let her get away with things like her dad did with her mother. She studied him and wrote down many things in her spiral notebook.

Mr. Hulse was the first teacher to give Mary straight A's all year. She did not know if she deserved them, but it challenged her to keep going. She must not be too much of a problem child if he gave her such high marks. She wanted to make him proud of her.

In that class it was easy to find bad traits, most of the boys were problem children. They were often pulled out and spanked by Mr. Hulse or the Principal. Mostly it was for not following directions. Mary decided if she ever got to know who The Unseen Voice was, she would follow His directions.

On Valentine's Day, Mary opened up her little Valentines from the class. One was not signed. It just said F--- you. Mary took it to Mr. Hulse during her lunch hour. He went through all of Mary's valentines and found they were all signed except for Allen's. He grabbed Allen, pulled him out of the class and spanked him with the Principal's paddle.

Mr. Hulse explain to Mary that boys who liked a girl sometimes did things like that valentine. They want the girl to pay attention to them. That was weird. Mary decided she would continue not paying any attention to Allen for the rest of her life.

Mr. Hulse had the class memorize the 23rd Psalm, "The Lord is my Shepherd." Each student would stand up and recite it to the class for their grade. That Psalm was a great comfort to Mary. Maybe The Unseen Voice was looking out after her and she would know Him some day as her Shepherd.

After saying the Pledge of Allegiance every morning over the speaker with the whole school, Mary's class continued by reciting the 23rd Psalms by themselves before they sat down.

They also memorized a poem by Rudyard Kipling:
"If you can keep your head when all about you
 Are losing theirs and blaming it on you,
If you can trust yourself when all men doubt you,
 And make allowance for their doubting too;
If you can wait and not be tired by waiting,
 Or being lied about, don't deal in lies,
Or being hated, don't give way to hating,
 And yet don't look too good, or talk too wise."

Mary took every word to heart. She wrote it down in her notebook and kept looking at it. She thought about everything that was wrong with her family towards her, and everything that was wrong with her towards her family. She needed more patience and to not treat her sister badly. She would try, no matter how bad things got.

The last day of school was sad because Mary would miss Mr. Hulse. Going to Junior High was scary. Mr. Hulse was just the kind of man Mary wanted to marry someday—Mr. Hulse and Uncle Jack--a combination of the two.

Between sixth and seventh grade Mary had a neighborhood friend named Pat who was a very good person. She had no brothers or sisters. Mary would spend the night at Pat's house and they would get into Pat's mother's expensive face cream.

Pat's dad was Pastor at a large Baptist Church. Pat invited Mary to Vacation Bible School, so she went. It was pretty good. Those Baptists memorized scripture and the stories were definitely not for babies.

The church bus came every day, picked up Pat and Mary, and brought them home. On the way home, the bus driver told everyone to bow their heads and close their eyes. He told them what it meant to accept Jesus into their hearts.

Mary did not understand what he was talking about. Maybe her mind was wandering because she did not want to go home. On the last day, she was the only one who had not raised her hand to accept Jesus. He kept driving and driving and talking and talking. In order to get home faster, she raised her hand. All the other kids clapped. They did not have their eyes closed. Perhaps they knew Mary was holding them up, or maybe they were happy she got "saved." She didn't know which.

Imagine Mary's horror when she looked out the window of her house that afternoon. Carol was in the yard wearing her shorts and halter top, smoking a cigarette and watering the grass. Pat's Pastor father was walking straight toward her. He told Carol how Mary got saved. Wouldn't she and her husband like to get saved so the family could all go to Heaven together?

Carol yelled for Mary to unsave herself and almost turned the water hose on the Pastor. Mary did not feel saved, so she was perfectly happy unsaving herself to get out of trouble. Pat's Pastor dad went home dejected.

When Mary went to her thirty-year high school reunion, she found out her friend Pat, her two sons, and Pat's next-door neighbor had been murdered by Pat's husband. He had gone to church, came home and tied them up using railroad spikes and wire on their arms and legs to hold them down and threw them in the river alive. The table was still set with dishes and dinner was in the oven.

Mary's heart broke thinking of what a good person Pat was, trying to do everything right. Yet life turned out so terrible for her and her children.

Mary heard that four women in her class had been murdered by their husbands. How horrifying! She wished she would have shared her spiral notebook with them and they would have found a good husband.

Seventh grade was the hardest year for Mary. Around Christmas she had emergency surgery to remove her appendix. When she was in the hospital, she got strep throat, but they did not know it. They thought it was a sore throat from the breathing tube. When she got home, she had Rheumatic Fever, an auto-immune disease from having strep, and was hospitalized for several months. She could not get out of bed because it could cause severe heart damage. She had the beginning of a heart murmur.

Her parents may have visited her in the hospital, but she could not remember one visit. She did remember a few short phone calls.

She lay in bed and tried to listen to her heart beating to see if she could tell how damaged it was. The more she listened, the more anxiety she felt. Before long, her heart was racing. She thought this disease was going to kill her but nobody wanted to tell her or cared.

Nobody ever told her much of anything. She was sure she would not be missed by anyone.

She was prescribed four aspirin every four hours day and night. They took so many blood samples from her arms that her veins collapsed. She was in a room all alone, not in pediatrics.

Mary was bored with nothing to do. Every day she grew weaker and weaker. She did not want to live as an invalid in bed when her family did not like her anyway. She decided to help this along.

Every time the nurse came with the four aspirin, she would only take three and hide one in her pillowcase. After she had a whole bunch of them, she took them all. She figured she had four hours to die. She closed her eyes to wait and wondered what it would be like. She could hear the evil voice laughing in her ears at each heartbeat. She could feel the black shadows on the ceiling dancing around.

She had a loud ringing in her ears which stopped her hearing the laughing and her heartbeat. Her stomach started hurting, but she tried not to thrown up the pills. The next she knew, a nurse was slapping her face and yelling her name.

Mary did not want to wake up, but the nurse was slapping harder and yelling louder. In Mary's mind she was yelling back, "Stop, stop, shut up!"

When she opened her eyes, she looked at the clock. It had only been two hours. Why did the nurse come back so soon? The doctor and nurse were scratching their heads. They decided they might have accidentally overdosed her.

They made her drink the most awful bottles of stuff Mary had ever tasted and they did not let her stop drinking for a long time. Mary had laid terrified in that bed all alone. The only thing she knew to do about it was kill herself.

She failed. Mary decided the next time she would not do it in the hospital where people watched you, slapped you, screamed your name, and made you drink awful stuff.

All that drink made her have to go to the bathroom. She decided she did not care if she died. She was getting out of bed instead of calling the nurse for a bedpan. She was going to walk down the hall to the bathroom by herself. She had enough of them!

Mary was so weak she held onto the walls to steady herself. When she got to the bathroom, she fainted and hit her head on the corner of a metal stall. It caused a gash in her head that bled all over.

When she came to, the same doctor and nurse were over her again, calling her name. This time they did not slap her. They helped her back to bed and cleaned her up.

They asked, "Why didn't you call for a nurse?" "Because I didn't want to!"

Mary's head reeled from taking the pills, and then fainting. The doctor decided not to put stitches in because the cut was not that big. He shaved off some of Mary's hair and put tape on her head. He then called her parents in the middle of the night on the phone next to her bed.

The doctor explained how Mary walked to the bathroom alone without ringing for the nurse, and fainted. (It was all Mary's fault.) He handed Mary the phone and her dad asked, "Did you break your glasses?"

"No."

She handed the phone back to the doctor. All he wanted to know was if this fainting was going to cost him anything.

When Mary was moved home, she was still bed-ridden for a while. Someone from her family opened the door, set a plate of food on her bed and closed the door. No speaking. They came back later and picked up the plate. Again, no speaking. It was very lonely. Her Aunt Agatha sent her some colored charcoals and a pad of paper to draw on. Mary appreciated that kindness.

When Mary was able to return to school, she took French because she was flunking Spanish. They were not so far along because their teacher did not know much French, but she made it fun.

Mary was also way behind in Algebra and when she sat in that class would feel like she was floating around the room and could not understand one thing the teacher said. She missed too much and always felt like she would have been good at math, but it got interrupted.

Mary never had to go to gym class again. No one was exactly sure how damaged her heart was and the doctor said, "No gym ever!" She remained on penicillin pills every day until she was an adult and got strep throat anyway. The Heart Association sent the pills free of charge. Her dad was happy about that, but this was just one more thing Mary worried about. If she got a sore throat, she worried it was strep. If her joints hurt, she thought she had rheumatic fever again.

Mary decided if her mother would not mother her, she would have to learn how to mother herself. She did not know what fathers were supposed to do. She thought they treat their daughters in a wise, loving, protective way. She could not do that for herself. Back in those days before divorce was popular, everyone had a father. She upgraded her list.

1. Never get addicted to anything
2. Treat people the way you want to be treated
3. Do good in school so you can get a job to support yourself so you can leave home when you graduate from high school
4. Do not have sex

That was a hard year. Being so sick with nobody visiting or caring changed Mary.

She had a heart for the hurting. A schoolmate and her brother were shot by her mother who then killed herself.

The children both survived. Mary visited them and took gifts several times so they would know somebody cared.

During eighth grade, President Kennedy was shot. It took a while to sink in. Mary was in her living room watching the news the next day when Lee Harvey Oswald got shot right as she sat there watching it live. She screamed because it was so shocking!

Mary could never understand the race riots she would see on the news at night. If she was older, she would go right down there and march with everyone. She loved Dr. Martin Luther King's speeches because she felt like an underdog herself. She wanted to know people who were different. She didn't know it then but one day she would get her chance.

A big storm was happening in Mary—inside and out. She did not know what to do about it. It made her sick inside.

STRENGTH AND WISDOM

When you are young, you don't know what happened to your parents to make them turn out the way they did.

Mary would find out later.

While Mary was at a band concert, Priscilla took money out of Jim's wallet. When she arrived home, everyone was screaming.

Carol turned to Mary and said, "When there is hell to pay, you are never around to get it! You are not eating with us for two weeks! Find your own place to eat!"

It took Mary a while to sort out this situation. Her sister got to eat with them although she was the one who stole the money. But because her dad yelled at Priscilla, Mary was punished for being at a band concert.

Nothing made sense. Carol protected Priscilla with her life. Jim could not yell at her! Carol was probably upset Mary had not been home so she could be blamed for stealing the money. If Carol was trying to get back at Jim for yelling at Priscilla, it did not work. He did not care if Mary was around or not.

For two weeks, Mary showed up at friends' houses to see if they would invite her to dinner. It was a mess. Mary told the story only to her Counselor at school. No one would believe it. Just another example that convinced Mary she was living in a crazy house and needed to get out. Mary could not understand how she could be so lonely living in a family of people.

Mary learned a lot about boys. She kept updating her list of traits. This study Mary was doing caused her to look at people in different ways. She looked deep to find people's essence. Popular, good looking, disabilities, or problems they encountered had nothing to do with how Mary saw people. She began to see something deeper.

But there was something else going on deep in her gut. She knew she was not alone in this world. Who was this Unseen Voice watching over her and saving her from herself? She could almost feel His hand in hers guiding her and walking with her. Was this somebody she was making up? He could not be made up, because when He said things to her, they were nowhere near what she was thinking. He was a wonder.

Mary brought home paperwork from her French class planning a trip to France over the summer with her teacher. Carol decided to send Priscilla instead. "You can go next year," Carol told Mary. Of course, the next year Mary did not go. Priscilla had not taken one day of French in her life. Why should Mary be surprised?

Mary kept on track taking business classes, typing faster and faster, learning shorthand and accounting. She became President of the Future Business Leaders of America, the largest club in her high school. With Mary's lists and standards, mothering herself was working. She tried to convince herself it did not matter that her parents never noticed her. What mattered was what she could do for herself. She was always working on herself so she could have a good life later since she had not had one yet. The depression was always with her. She went to school counselors to unload her burden. She hardly ever went to parties, but when she did, she did not drink, smoke or have sex.

Mary was still a horse lover. Where her love for horses came from, she had no idea. She felt she was born with it.

She had no hope of ever owning a big beautiful horse, but she never let go of that dream.

A boy in Mary's class showed up at her house on Saturday mornings with two horses saddled and ready to go.

Mary ran out and jumped on one and they rode for hours.

Another friend's dad bought a retired race horse that was pregnant as an investment. What a beautiful mare! Mary had never seen such a horse. When they got her home and put her in the stable, her dad said, "You girls stay off her. She's a race horse and you could get hurt."

They did not listen. They sneaked out to ride her around inside the fence. She was no trouble at all. She walked, trotted a little bit, and seemed to enjoy the exercise. They watched her belly grow and saw her foal.

Mary had another friend who was afraid of her own horse, but Mary wanted to see him. She talked her friend's dad into letting her ride him. Everything was going good until the horse was stung by a wasp on his backside. He jumped straight up in the air and took off at a full gallop.

She gave him the reigns and let him go. He headed straight for the creek galloping full speed through the field. Mary squeezed her knees into his sides, kept the reigns loose, put her head down on his neck, and let him jump the creek. She never had so much fun in her life. When she jumped him back over the creek and came into her friend's front yard, the dad's face was completely white. He could not believe Mary did not fall off.

Her best friend, Cindy was in Westernairs Horse Capade and Mary rode and tended her horse with her.

After riding all her friend's horses, Mary became a good rider. She loved having all that power under her doing what she wanted the horse to do. Mary never fell off or felt fear. When she was on a horse, she felt free like a girl with no problems in the world.

Housework was a hard for Mary. She was yelled at to do something, but not shown how to do it. It was always punishment, and her goal was to get away from the house as much as possible so they couldn't find her. They did not care or notice her unless they had work for her to do. It was the best she could do at that time. Priscilla couldn't help because she said her hands were allergic to water.

Mary would dream of her ideal job. It would be somewhere she could work day and night and never have to come home.

Almost every day, Mary was sent to the grocery store to buy something for dinner and get her mom cigarettes. Over the summer she met a boy working there who was one year older than her. He was quite smitten with Mary. They started dating but Mary was still studying traits. The object was not just getting any old boy.

Everything went fine for a while. He took her to homecoming and treated her well, but she noticed he was getting more and more controlling. One thing that was not going to happen was Mary being controlled all her adult life.

He wanted people to know he had a good-looking girlfriend. In chemistry class he sat by Dennis and wrote Mary notes. Dennis would say, "Tell Mary I said hi". Mary wrote back, "Tell Dennis hi". This went back and forth for a long time.

Mary did not know who Dennis was but wanted to find out. The first time she saw him, he had on tan cords, a madras shirt, and tiger striped socks. He had light brown eyes, and well-kept brown hair. The socks made her curious. He was about the same height as Mary (but ended up being six-foot tall), was not a jock or into organized sports. He cared about his studies, and was a little shy. He loved the mountains to hunt and fish with his dad.

Mary kept him in the back of her mind as someone she wanted to get to know better. She noticed he had this look that was indescribable. When he liked what you said, it would just show up for a few seconds--especially in his eyes. A look of approval that made Mary feel good.

Mary could tell a lot about a person by looking at their eyes. She did not know how this worked, but she knew it was right.

As her boyfriend became more and more controlling, he told Mary what to wear on certain dates or talked about "When we are married. " Mary started planning how to break up with him.

One day he was at Mary's house playing basketball on her driveway. He picked her up and threw her over his shoulder so she couldn't beat him to the ball. He was big and strong, but that was the straw that broke the camel's back. Big and strong was not exactly something she was looking for, and he hurt her in the process. Mary was competitive. If she beat him, she beat him.

When he went home, she called him and said they were done. He pleaded and pleaded, but Mary stuck to her guns. He came back to her house to change her mind, but she would not let him in or unlock the screen door. She had become a little afraid of him.

She did not give him any specific reason why. She just said she was not ready for a relationship where he was making plans for their future. He said he was going to tell all his friends that she had sex with him so they would not date her.

"Go ahead," Mary said, and slammed the door. She knew she made a good decision to dump him.

She was worried about him spreading untrue rumors with a group of guys that included Dennis. Mary did not want them to think of her as a slut.

Two weeks later on Halloween night, the phone rang and Jim Jr. said, "It's a Dennis." She went to the phone and he asked her out on a date. She said "Yes."

Silence, then he said, "You will?"

"Yes." That was it. They said "goodbye" and hung up.

They started seeing each other a little between classes. He was cute and had some maturity about him. He did not do stupid things to get a girl's attention. Mary was impressed. He was a sophomore and she was a freshman but only two months apart in age. He started school in first grade and skipped kindergarten. They started looking like a couple.

A lot of girls in his class started giving Mary dirty looks as if she was stealing "one of theirs." Mary just ignored them and waited to go on their first date. Waiting made it that much more interesting.

Mary heard the Unseen Voice say, "Be strong, Mary, be strong." She had heard those words many times in the past when people were against her.

Their first date finally arrived. They decided to go to the Paramount Theater and see *The Fortune Cookie*.

When Dennis came to the door to pick Mary up, Mary's grandma and grandpa were visiting. As they were walking down the sidewalk to get into his car, Mary's grandma said, "Why are you letting her go out with that short boy?" For the first time in her life, Mary was mad at her grandma. Dennis acted like he didn't hear it but Mary knew he did. Mary was confused. Would her grandma like it better if she was going out with a tall boy? Probably not. She just did not want her to go out at all.

They held hands during the movie. He was a gentleman, opening the doors for her and treating her well. He was moving higher and higher on Mary's list of traits. They went to a burger place (King's on West Colfax) where all the Jefferson County students from different schools congregated after dates or sporting events.

They ate and talked and tried to get to know each other. Dennis asked Mary if she was Catholic. "No." He had noticed she was wearing a cross with a little diamond in it. One of her former boyfriends had given it to her for Christmas and she liked it. They finished eating, Dennis paid the whole bill (check off one trait) and they went out to get in his red stick-shift Corvair.

Mary noticed he was not taking her home. He was headed for Lookout Mountain, or "Make-out Mountain" as it was commonly called. It went up quickly and twisty, climbing a two-lane road outside of Golden. Driving on the snow in a light car was tricky, especially with cars coming down the other way from 3.2 beer clubs. Dennis parked the car where couples came for privacy, and they looked out and saw all of Denver's city lights. It was beautiful with the new-fallen snow.

They sat there for a few minutes taking in the view. Then Dennis turned to Mary and said, "For two weeks I have been wondering what it would be like to kiss you." He leaned over and kissed her. One kiss. He started his car, took her home and walked her to the door.

Man-oh-man, that was the sweetest kiss Mary ever had. She just knew Dennis was the one. He reminded her of Uncle Jack and Mr. Hulse. In fact, after the date she cried because she was afraid of getting hurt. She was serious about this boy.

Mary could not wait until they could get together again. She realized she had missed one thing on character and traits. Love. She had no idea what it was, because she had never felt love for someone or been loved. Was love when you were looking for his face in a crowd, even though it was ridiculous he would be there? That was happening.

Mary had never experienced anything like this and realized there was a good chance she could get hurt to the core. She was young and just wanted to have fun and study boys. But she decided to take that chance. If she got hurt, she would just have to learn how to get over it.

She hoped Dennis was the one because he was who she wanted. They were both only 16. Mary decided it was better to find the right person at the wrong time, than the wrong person at the right time. She also noticed when she saw him walking down the hall at school, she had this feeling she could not explain. Excitement? Love? It was different than she ever felt before. He was a keeper.

Mary confided in Dennis some of the problems she had at home and he confided in her some problems he had.

One night, Dennis drove over to Mary's house. In a calm voice he told her parents, "You are not treating Mary right. You favor her sister and brother. She deserves to be treated better."

Mary was mortified. This 16-year-old boy was standing up to her parents to protect her. Of course, she got hell from them when he left. "What are you telling him about us? Nothing leaves this house!"

But he had shown Mary he did love her, or he would never have confronted them. He wanted to keep her from the hurt her family was dumping on her, even if it didn't work. Good trait!

They dated all through high school. Mary's old boyfriend was mad as hell that he ever introduced his girlfriend to Dennis. It would not have mattered. Mary would have broken up with him anyway. He would call every now and then to express his anger. Mary kept it short. Over is over. He had their whole future planned out, but it was not Mary's plans.

Dennis and Mary bought matching blue ski sweaters with a white stripe down the arms. They wore them to school every Friday just in case anybody had any doubts about where they stood.

Early Saturday mornings, Dennis would go to Mary's in his dad's red Willy jeep. They would head for the mountains. Dennis loved the mountains and he especially loved exploring every dirt road he came to. No one knew the Western slope like Dennis.

Mary packed egg salad sandwiches and a thermos of hot chocolate. They shot the guns, and hiked. Mary collected rocks and Dennis carried them back to the jeep. They looked for wildlife and enjoyed nature. Since Dennis was color-blind, he could spot shapes of deer and elk on the next mountain. He pointed them out to Mary. She strained and finally saw them.

Dennis could see fish under the water which made him an excellent fly fisherman. Mary could only see the reflection on top of the water. He said, "There is a big trout over by that rock."

Then he swung his grandfather's fly rod back and forth a couple of times. The fly beautifully kissed the water right by the rock and bam! He had the trout.

Mary thought it was amazing because she thought *"No fish in this stream."* She was very pessimistic about fishing.

They had one problem. Mary would not go to the bathroom anywhere but home. She would not go in the woods, in an outhouse, or at a dirty old gas station. Dennis sometimes had to drive Mary all the way home, she would run into the house, go to the bathroom, run back out and they would head back up to the mountains. That was a strange nuisance to Dennis because he had been going to the bathroom in the woods since he was five. He kept trying to change Mary's mind and coerce her into not having to go home, but it was to no avail.

During bad snow storms, Dennis picked up Mary. They drove to an empty mall parking lot and turned donuts in the jeep. It was quite fun and exciting. While everyone stayed out of the snow, they went directly for it. Even though Denver's snows were dangerous, they were beautiful and romantic. The crystals were dry and sparkled like diamonds in the parking lot lights.

Sometimes they went to Genesee Park and found a picnic table with a fire pit to roast hot dogs for dinner and stay warm. They talked for hours.

Dennis' dad was in the Army during World War II and was a stickler on gun safety. He taught Dennis at an early age. He landed on Normandy Beach D-day plus five. He was shot twice, given antibiotics, but sent on. From France, he made it to Germany. He was a tough old guy and Mary was sure he gave those Germans hell, although he never talked about it.

When he came home, he was not the same person as when he left. He had seen too much, experienced too much as young man. He was only happy in the mountains with his youngest son, Dennis. He drank too much to relieve the pain. He lost the love and respect of his family, except for Dennis--the one Mary wanted.

Dennis graduated from high school, leaving Mary behind to finish her senior year alone. He went to the Colorado School of Mines in Golden at 17. His dad wanted him to become an engineer and live at home. He never helped pay for any schooling, but did buy Dennis a new white Chevy Malibu for high school graduation.

Dennis was the first one in his family to go to college. The college was within walking distance to the Coors Brewery. Dennis walked over, ate his lunch in their cafeteria and got a free beer to boot. Nice break after taxing your brain all morning with that engineering stuff.

Since he lived at home, Dennis was strict about his study time. He studied every weeknight, then picked Mary up from high school on Friday. They would hang out all day Saturday. Then Dennis studied all day Sunday.

Not being with Dennis as much caused tension in Mary. She was around the house she hated even more. Her sister was going to Patricia Stephens Modeling and Finishing School and became a pom-pom girl for the Air Force Academy. She met a gorgeous football player and they started dating. She lived at home, too. The pom-pom Queen.

One-night Dennis and Mary got in a fight and broke up. She knew this could happen. It was because of the tension of not seeing each other enough. She had so many things in her bedroom that reminded her of him, and he had so many things of hers. She wanted her framed school book picture back.

Mary called Dennis, "Can we talk about working things out and getting back together?" "No." "Then I'm coming over to get my things."

Mary went to Dennis' house. She walked right into his bedroom, head held high, and started picking things up.

None of his family would speak to her.

Dennis stood in the bedroom doorway and watched her. She took her picture and a few other things she had given him because "he was the one." No tears, just being logical. Tears would come later. She had business to do.

When she got home, Mary called her friend Cindy to see if she could come and help clean out her room of all of his things. Mary had pictures and poems they had written each other and a lot of his stuff that needed to go if she had any hope of recovering and starting over.

Cindy said, "Sure, but Why don't you come over here, help me clean house, and then we'll hit your bedroom?" It was a plan. Mary drove to Cindy's house.

Cindy had moved to Bear Creek and was no longer living within walking distance of Mary's house.

As they were cleaning the house, the doorbell rang. Dennis was standing on the front porch. He had no idea where Cindy lived. He had driven all through Bear Creek searching for Mary's car.

He came in the house and stood in the hallway. He said to Mary, "After you left and took your picture, I could not imagine my life without you. I went to Zales and purchased an engagement ring with two wedding bands. Here's the receipt, because your ring is being sized. Will you marry me?"

He made it clear their marriage would not be any time soon, but it would be a forever thing. He stood there waiting, unsure what Mary's answer would be.

"Yes!" Mary checked the receipt to be sure. She was happy. No tears in the near future. Her plan was still intact. Mary followed Dennis back to her house. She gave her "fiancé" her stuff back, and they went out for the day.

They decided not to tell anyone they were engaged until the ring was on her finger.

Dennis planned to finish the semester at Colorado School of Mines, then quit because he did not want to be an engineer. He wanted to go to CU Denver Center to the School of Business. He had already talked to his mom about it and she was on board, although his dad would hit the roof.

That meant he and Mary would have more time together. She could hardly wait. Mary would be engaged her last year of high school and see Dennis more. A sparkly diamond had Mary walking on clouds.

Carol and Jim were happy for Mary and Dennis. Dennis' family was not so happy about the news. His father, looked at the diamond said, "Shit," turned around and walked away. His mother did not want to lose her baby, the only one still at home.

Mary knew she would help Dennis reach his dream of being the first college-educated person in his family. She wanted to go to college but in those days, you couldn't get a grant if your parents made too much money. Hers did. They had no intention of spending any of it on her.

They had bought her brother a new Mustang, then a new Mustang GT while he was still in high school and two years later, a very expensive new Ford Italian Pantera. Priscilla got gowns to go to Air Force dances after the football games. Mary was not jealous of things. She wanted their love and for them to "know" her.

Taking out her own loan for school went against Mary's plans for saving money. She would work and Dennis would go to school. But she always knew in her heart she would have made a darn good prosecuting attorney.

One night close to graduation, someone from the school called to speak to Carol. Mary had been selected for National Honor Society and was graduating in the top four percent of her class. An all-school ceremony was planned followed by a tea with the parents. After the tea, the students could go home with their parents and not finish the day at school. This was to be a surprise for Mary.

As soon as Carol hung up the phone, she started yelling. "I can't take off work for this. No, I won't be at your National Honor Society induction." The only one in her family that was happy for Mary was Aunt Doris. She had made National Honor Society 25 years earlier and knew what an honor it was.

Mary heard her name announced, went up to get her pin and gold tassel for her graduation cap (everyone else had a black tassel), then walked back and sat down. When the assembly was over, Mary skipped the tea and finished all her classes. Oh, to have parents that could be happy for her just once, to help her enjoy her achievements and take an afternoon off work to celebrate how Mary had worked hard all through high school.

Mary had learned not to retaliate when her family hurt her. She kept her mouth shut and just kept going. This would be helpful later.

Two weeks after Mary graduated from high school, her parents went on a trip. Dennis came over one night.

Priscilla asked Mary to go get her something from the store.

Dennis had enough. He said, "You don't have a broken leg, and you are not retarded. Go yourself!"

When Mary's parents came home her sister gave them an earful of how Dennis treated her. They told him to leave and never come back to their house again. Seriously? Kicking Mary's fiancé out of the house?

Mary turned to Dennis and said, "Wait, I'm coming with you!" This was her chance. She went into the bedroom and picked the only three dresses she could claim as her own, and took her hair dryer.

A meager beginning. As she closed the front door behind her, she could not think of one meaningful conversation she had with anyone in her family in the last 18 years. So sad. No one there to share anything with. Nothing but loneliness. She left with Dennis and stayed at his house for two weeks.

Mary had stolen forks, knives and spoons from the school lunch room. She felt so bad about it she told her counselor what she had done. He laughed and absolved her of the theft. "They accidentally throw more than that away every day. Keep them."

Mary had a government job lined up with the Bureau of Reclamation in the typing pool but she needed to wait until she received her first check. She bought a very cheap car and made payments. She found an apartment for $89 a month and put a deposit on it. When she moved in, the people had left a lot of their furniture behind. not great, but it was a start.

Mary's life-long dream of being on her own was happening. She was not sure she could make it financially, but she had to try. Her feelings swirled with fear, happiness, despair, and hope.

The Unseen Voice said, "You can do this, Mary!"

She had no idea who she was when she was alone in her apartment. She only knew who she had to be to survive all those years. How and where do you find yourself when you've been completely invisible, walking on eggshells so no one would yell at you?

She had anger and shame that cut deep. She held in so many secrets from her friends about who she really was. There was always that "other voice" that made her think the real reason she was not being loved was because she was not lovable.

One of the demands for herself was to never get addicted to anything, but she started cursing like everybody else she worked with. The anger came out ugly and profane. She dropped a few F-bombs at her mother and sister. She told them to "Go to hell!" When Mary cursed, she was not invisible. It created a lot of attention. Of course, she did not know what "hell" really was or she would never have said it. Mary did not like who she was becoming.

She would try to control the cursing around Dennis, but she was addicted. The more she tried, the worse it became. What was she going to do? Who knew you could get addicted to such a thing?

Dennis picked up Mary for a ride in the mountains. It was spring, but had snowed. Dennis drove up the mountain while Mary sat right next to him. Again, no seat belts. As they rounded a curve, they came to a place sheltered by the mountain shade with no sun to melt the ice.

They hit a patch of black ice. Their car swerved over into the oncoming lane. As the wheels grabbed the dry pavement, the car turned straight for the edge of the highway, heading off the mountain at a high rate of speed. Suddenly a guardrail caught them. They bumped their heads, but nothing serious. Behind the spiritual curtain, the devil was trying his best to get rid of Mary, but nothing worked. That was the only guardrail on the mountain at that time.

Both Dennis and Mary knew they would have been dead had that guardrail not stopped them. No one would have found them down the mountain in the trees. Mary thanked The Unseen Voice for saving their lives again.

On a beautiful day in late August, in a Catholic Church with 100 people attending, Dennis and Mary made their eternal vows to each other in front of a crotchety old priest.

The first time they went in to talk to him, he was drinking whiskey and smoking. Mary did not think he was a Christian in those black robes. He told them how to get married by the Catholic Book. Mary could tell he had no love in his heart and certainly did not share their excitement. She decided that the Catholic church needed a cleansing. Little did she know.

Dennis had been raised Catholic and even though he was agnostic, he was still afraid if he entered another church something terrible would happen to him.

Mary's plan since the fifth grade was becoming reality. The old priest told Mary she had to take Catechism classes and be sprinkled as a Catholic. Both Dennis and Mary had to take marriage classes for 12 weeks. A cool, younger priest taught the classes. Mary thought he way too good looking to be a priest. What would a priest know about marriage anyway?

The priest said, "Look around at this class. In 12 weeks, one-third of you will break up because this class will expose you to what marriage really is." Mary hoped it would not be them. They learned about in-law problems, money management, dividing holidays, handling disagreements, having children before being ready, and how to split up home chores. They had a doctor come and discussed sexual intercourse.

The priest gave the most important advice ever, "Never, lie to each other or your marriage won't be a marriage." And, "Never speak ill of your spouse to other people. If you have a problem with them, go to them directly. You are one."

Dennis and Mary both listened intently. It was all good. They already knew some of the problems they would face. It was good to remember about the importance of the the marriage and not just the wedding. Actually, the wedding only meant that Mary was finally going to become Mrs. Dennis which she had waited three years for.

The classes came to an end. They were not in the one-third that gave up. Mary was sprinkled Catholic to get married in the Catholic church, her second baptism. She convinced the old Priest she would have many children, not use birth control, and raise them all Catholic. She lied.

Dennis had to go to confession after 11 years of being agnostic. He would not talk about it. It was private.

Mary did not go to confession because she was still confused about sin. She told God she did not honor her father and her mother, and coveted something somebody else had--a loving family. She just left it at that--out of The Ten Commandments.

Mary went alone and rented the first wedding gown she tried on for $60. She paid for it herself. It was lace with a mantilla headpiece and a long train in the back. All that mattered was it was beautiful to Mary. No family or friends went with her. She handed over three

$20 bills and signed the agreement wondering how many brides had worn this exact same dress.

Mary struggled over what to carry down the aisle. Instead of a bouquet of flowers, she bought a white Bible. She had a flower shop put a live yellow orchid on top. The color yellow meant courage and personal power. Mary had never seen this before, or since. She knew was this was a special book. Maybe The Unseen Voice put it in her heart.

Mary was a thin young blonde with long hair that flipped at the ends. She knew for once everybody would be looking at her. She was a beautiful girl. The dress she picked, size 4, accentuated her figure and face. The photographer was a friend of Jim's and offered to take the wedding pictures for free.

Mary did have her one and only good time with her younger brother. He was excited for her to get married. They had a connection for just a couple of days. Mary and her brother never had a connection again. It was God's wedding gift to give her that touch for her wedding.

Cindy and another friend stood up with Mary with her sister being the maid of honor with a frown on her face because Mary beat her to the altar.

It was a simple cheap wedding. No rehearsal dinner, just sandwiches at Jim and Carol's. The church was not decorated with flowers. The reception was in a small rented conference room at a Holiday Inn. No music at the reception. It was all they could afford, but it was enough for Dennis and Mary. Neither family offered to pitch in. This wedding had nothing to do with any dreams anyone had for these two getting married.

No one was happy except for Dennis and Mary. Mary's smiling glow made up for everything! She was not going to let anyone ruin her day. Dennis looked so handsome in a black tux. He had been working for the County Parks that summer and had quite a tan. Mary was so happy to get the one she wanted and not have to settle or live the rest of her life alone.

Dennis' mother cried, and they were not tears of joy. She was losing her baby boy. Mary's grandma and aunts were mad because Mary was getting married in "that" Catholic Church.

Jim walked Mary down the aisle. It was one of her good moments with her dad. You can't ignore a daughter in a wedding gown on your arm in front of 100 people. He was sweet. She even noticed a few tears in his eyes.

Even though the priest told them her dad could not say anything, he said, "I give you, my daughter, to Dennis to marry." He didn't say it for everyone to hear, he said it to Mary.

Mary kissed his cheek, then turned to Dennis, took his hand and was his forever.

Mary's grandpa had passed away from colon cancer, but Grandma said she saw him up on stage blessing Mary and Dennis during the service. Whether she did or not, it was good because Mary did not want to do anything to hurt the people she loved by not marrying in a Protestant church.

The only person Mary saw was Dennis with his light brown eyes looking only at her with his expression of approval.

Mary felt the curtain open a crack and saw heavenly joy at the end of the ceremony. Happiest day of her life!

Mary whispered "Amen".

The Priest had forbidden the kiss at the rehearsal. Mary figured he would not slap her in front of all these people like he did her friend at their rehearsal. But Mary did back up a half a step. She was worried he would not sign the Marriage Certificate, but he did and groused off. This was her one and only wedding and that old man was not going to keep her from kissing her new husband!

After the small reception, they hit I-70 west for their honeymoon. They headed for Glenwood Springs for three days. Mary had to get back to work, and Dennis could not miss school. They stayed at a Travel Lodge Motel, drove around, Dennis fished, Mary read books, and they soaked in the mineral pool at night. With the snow coming down, it was breathtaking.

They drove to Aspen for a day to look in shops they could not afford and had lunch.

On one of their drives on a dirt road they spotted a horse ranch. They stopped and asked if they could rent two horses for a day ride. "No." the owner said. "We're getting the horses and gear ready for the hunting season starting next week."

But his wife saw "Just Married" on their back window. She talked her husband into letting them take the horses without a guide. Her husband saddled up two good horses. Mary and Dennis rode into forest for an afternoon of honeymoon bliss. Riding those horses made everything perfect for Mary, another gift from The Unseen Voice. The wife would not let them pay.

The Vietnam War was going full force. With a low draft number of 56, they knew Dennis would get drafted. But their wedding and honeymoon was everything Mary planned for since the fifth grade and she was not going to let a war a million miles away spoil their special honeymoon days.

TWO BECOME ONE

Mary's apartment became their apartment. She was no longer alone. Back to school, back to work. Mary worked all the overtime possible. She typed thesis' and college papers to make extra money. And she typed all of Dennis' papers.

As she excelled in her work, she climbed to supervisor for The Office for Equal Opportunity. Women and minority movements were gaining a voice in Congress. They were marching against the status quo.

Mary's cooking left a lot to be desired. When she lived by herself, dinner might be a can of corn. Dennis wanted real meals. His brother-in-law was Italian and felt sorry for Dennis. He taught Mary how to make Italian dishes. She could not understand a cook book. Band and choir kept her out of home economics. What did "T" or "t" mean? What did "cream" mean? She did not understand recipes. She followed her co-workers home to watch and learn as they baked cookies. She began to improve.

As Mary drove out of the government complex one afternoon, she heard a man's voice yell, "STOP!" She had the green light, but the voice was so loud, she literally stood up on the brake pedal. A VW mini-van ran a red light, music blaring. It would have crashed right into Mary's door killing her for sure.

She sat there shaking and looked in the backseat. No one was there. The Unseen Voice had saved her life again. She thanked Him, whoever He was, and shook all the way home. She thought about The Unseen Voice always being a part of her life, but she still did not know who He was. But he was always there when she needed help.

Mary's sister married her fiancé in a beautiful ceremony at the Air Force Academy Chapel on graduation day, complete with swords, white military uniforms, and stained-glass windows. It was breathtaking. She wore a gorgeous wedding dress adorned with Australian crystals. After Mary walked down the aisle and turned around to watch her sister on her dad's arm, it took her breath away.

She was so beautiful like a princess marrying her prince. Their reception was at The Four Seasons—quite different than Mary's wedding.

They were stationed in Arizona for flight school. Carol gave Mary a ticket to go see how they were doing. It was Mary's first time on an airplane. Half-way to Arizona the plane lost an engine and flew lopsided, first to the right then to the left. They prepared the runway for a crash landing, but the plane landed with no problems. The Unseen Voice again saving Mary?

Life went on. Dennis graduated from college with his Business Degree, which was his dad's pride and joy. Although his dad never once helped pay for any of the schooling, he sent Dennis and Mary on a trip to Hawaii for a week of relaxing in the sun.

In August of 1972, Dennis went to the Post Office to pick up something that was certified while Mary went to the doctor because she was not feeling well. They both came home with news. Dennis was drafted and Mary was pregnant. Scary times were ahead.

They considered Canada, but Dennis' dad would strongly object. They found a doctor who for 50 dollars, would find something "wrong" with you to keep you out of the Army. The day he was supposed to testify for Dennis, the doctor died. They were stuck between Army or jail.

Mary had morning sickness so bad she quit work and went to live with her parents, something she said she would never do. Mary laid in bed and sucked on lime popsicles. It was a lot easier being with her parents when she was their only child at home.

Mary drove Dennis to the Army Induction Center to get farmed out to boot camp. Then Mary and her little belly went downtown to the May Company and got her ears pierced, something Dennis never wanted her to do. She never wanted him to go to the Army either. Rebellion.

She stood in line with pre-teen girls with smiles on their faces. They gave Mary confidence. This was going to be a piece of cake. When it was her turn, it hurt so bad she started crying. She thought about leaving, but what good would one pierced ear do? She bought a pair of sterling silver earrings to fill the holes and decided not to tell Dennis. He had enough on his mind. He could figure it out when and if he ever came home.

Dennis called Mary from boot camp and told her he was sick, could not stop coughing and had a fever. Dennis never got sick. He was stationed at Rolla, Missouri, and they had been trying to get rid of the Acute Respiratory Disease (ARD) for years! He had been peeling potatoes all day.

Mary made the big mistake of telling her mother. Carol called her Senator. Her last name was pronounced exactly the same as the presiding Speaker of the House. They jumped at her command. Immediately a Senate investigation started at Fort Leonard Wood as to why Dennis would be peeling potatoes with the ARD.

The next morning Dennis was called out of roll call into the Base Commander's office. "Private, do you call your mother-in-law every time you are sick?" "No, sir. I told my wife." "Report to sick bay and do not peel any more potatoes, do you hear me?" "Yes, sir."

It might have been a good thing in disguise. *Handle this soldier with care.*

After Basic Training he was assigned to New Jersey where they called Coke soda and spaghetti sauce gravy. Everyone had a funny accent. He was a Personnel Specialist. With his college degree in business, he would read the regulations and statutes and interpret them for the brass. At least he wasn't shooting at people or getting shot.

In the middle of February, Mary came to New Jersey. They rented an efficiency apartment on the Jersey shore and hunkered down to wait for their furniture. Everything on the boardwalk was closed for winter. Their apartment was drafty cold and had no phone. With her big belly, Mary had to walk up and down slippery icy stairs.

Mary's mother got to drinking and called the White House asking for Nixon in the middle of the night. Because of her last name, they got an aide out of bed and on the phone. She said, "Nixon drafted my son-in-law and now my daughter is with him and eight months pregnant. I want to know where she is right now!"

The White House Aide woke up Dennis' Base Commander. He called the MPs to go up and down the Jersey Shore looking for Mary. At three in the morning they heard a pounding on the door. An MP yelled, "Mary, are you in there?" "Yes, sir." "You call your mother right away!"

Mary thought someone had died. They dressed to go out into the blowing snow off the ocean and drove around to find a phone booth. Mary's mom picked up the phone and in a very nice voice said, "Oh hi. I was just wondering where you were." The conversation was short. She was no longer calling principals and teachers. Now it was Senators and Presidents.

The next morning Dennis had to report to his new Base Commander. "Private?" "Yes, sir!" "You have your wife report to her mother where she is at all times." "Yes, sir!"

Fort Monmouth, where Dennis was stationed, had a hospital on base. It was where the POWs were released from captivity in Vietnam. The war was over. We lost. The hospital was packed with men who looked like the walking dead. Mary was thankful Dennis was not among them. It was sad. They were her age or younger.

Mary was eight months pregnant had to go to the base hospital every Friday at eight a.m. every week. Every pregnant woman from Fort Monmouth checked in at the same time. They called the women according to their husband's rank. Unfortunately, Dennis was the lowest rank in the military. Mary waited four hours, worried and homesick.

Her baby was okay, but she was a crying, depressed mess. The doctor wrote a prescription to report to the Psych Ward. She yelled

"My husband ~~was drafted by Nixon.~~ I am eight months pregnant and hundreds of miles from home. I have no friends. I have been sitting here since eight a.m. this morning. Wouldn't you be damn depressed?"

Th doctor let her leave. She was not all right, either.

Mary knew nothing about having a baby, and how this bowling ball in her belly was going to get out. They found birthing and La Leche classes.

Mary decided she was going to have this baby naturally because it was the safest thing for the baby. She would never forgive herself if there was something wrong with her baby because She was a nervous mess.

Epidurals were not perfected and were risky. A big "no." on that. Just breathe the Lamaze way and softly rub your screaming belly. She prepared herself to endure the pain and do what she had to do. She did not care about hurting herself. She wanted to be awake and see her baby right after birth, not wake up later like her mother.

On March 12, 1973, Mary woke up to strong contractions. Her first instinct was to get into a warm bathtub. Dennis left for work because the birthing coach said it would be a long time, maybe not until tomorrow. Mary tried to wash dishes, but it was too hard with the labor pains.

As she looked out the window, she saw Dennis pulled into his parking place. He realized he should be home with Mary.

Mary heard Dennis call the maternity ward, "Are you busy today?" She felt like a car he was taking in for minor repairs. Who cared if they were busy? This baby was coming.

For a first baby, this labor was moving fast.

"Dennis, if you don't get me to the hospital right now, I'm going to have this baby right here in our bed!"

He helped Mary in the car and started driving. Mary thought he hit every bump in the road. At one stoplight, she counted three contractions.

At the hospital she was already dilated to a nine. One more centimeter and she could start pushing.

The doctor thought she should have a C-section because her pelvis was too small. "No, I want to do this myself." She started pushing.

The doctor said, "I have to move the baby's head down to dislodge it from your pelvic bone. Are you sure you don't want to be put to sleep? This is really going to hurt."

"No."

He took a big spoon-like thing and shoved it up and moved the baby's head down. Pain you could not believe. During the next contractions Mary was able to push her baby out. He was a beautiful baby boy with plenty of hair. Mary had never seen such a gorgeous perfect baby.

Dennis was not allowed in the delivery room but the door had accidentally been left open. He stood just outside the door, watched and listened. He saw his baby as soon as the doctor held him up.

Mary did not scream, groan, or curse, like women do on TV or in the movies when they're in labor. She was focused, concentrating and very fixated on what she was doing. The only noise she made was to ask for an ice chip.

They cleaned up her healthy baby boy and placed him beside her bed. From this point on, she was responsible for his care. They told her where to get what she needed. She was in a fog.

Dennis and Mary marveled at this new human being. Mary did not know how to care for baby. It was hard for her to get out of bed, pick him up and climb back in the old Army bed high off the floor and not adjustable. She had pushed so hard, she felt her bottom was going to drop right out and land on the floor.

For first-time babies, it was a 10-day mandatory stay. Worse, Dennis could only see Mary and his new son twice a day for one hour each time. Army Regulations. When he came, Mary had a list of things for him to help her. The bed sheets needed changing, bathroom needed cleaning, climb on a chair and change the TV channel, walk a block long hall and replace the supplies she was running out of.

Mary was careful not to complain to her mom. Who would Carol call about this? The Pope? Dennis was an agnostic Catholic.

Mary was required to go to a meeting every day, pushing her heavy Army chair from her room to the meeting and sit on it for an hour with her stitches screaming. The first instructions were about Vaseline someplace, rubbing alcohol somewhere else, something would fall off in about a week, steal a brush from the Army somewhere to brush hard enough someplace to prevent cradle cap (whatever that was). She decided not to do any of it because she might put the wrong thing in the wrong place and the wrong thing would fall off. Her ears were still ringing from pushing. She also broke many blood vessels in her face, and her stitches were screaming sitting on that chair.

Mary had to walk a block to get her own meals and carry the tray back, shuffling between the army soldiers. It was exhausting. She would take off everything she wouldn't eat or didn't need. She also had to take it back and thought about throwing some plates away for the long walk.

Dennis was a trooper and helped Mary as much as possible. He was a daddy and if the Army made him depressed, his son made him happy. His first words when he saw him from the doorway of the delivery room were, "There is a God!"

Finally, the 10-day sentence was over and Mary and baby were released.

Her parents came and really liked the baby. In fact, they really liked Mary for giving them a beautiful grandson. Their relationship was healing.

Carol was not a good cook, but great at finding take-out. They ate delicious seafood and Italian food. Breads were scrumptious, Old World recipes. Fish was fresh, not frozen. They ate well.

Jim went out and bought the baby a beautiful crib with a Simmons mattress. He believed good mattresses were important. Mary never knew that, because she did not grow up with good mattresses. She learned many years later that her dad never had a bed or a mattress when he was growing up and never had enough food. He had to sleep on a sofa. They also brought baby presents from the people Carol worked with.

They left and Carol was a great help with more knowledge than Mary imagined. It was a good time alone with her mom and baby while Dennis was at work.

When Mary's baby was 3-months old, Mary and baby watched Secretariat race on TV. He won the Kentucky Derby, the Preakness and the Belmont Stakes shattering all records. No other horse had a chance. In his autopsy, his heart was three times larger than a normal race-horse. He got much more oxygen to his body. Mary knew in her heart The Unseen Voice made him for her to enjoy while holding her baby and watching a woman from Denver believe in her horse. The horse is the only animal God created to run into a battle instead of running away from it. They have no fear. They know how strong they are. Mary wanted to be that strong. She wanted her children to be that strong. Secretariat was the first triple-crown winner in Mary's lifetime. She just knew her boys would be good runners.

Her baby did not do things by the book. He never crawled. At six months old he would pull himself up to hold onto something, turn and start running until he fell or got where he wanted to go. If he fell, he got back up and tried again and again. He was always wanting to do things that frustrated him.

Dennis was just the kind of husband Mary had been dreaming about finding and now they had the start of their little family. He always supported anything Mary wanted to do. He was never selfish or self-serving. He never lied or gossiped or said one bad thing about anybody. He was a wonderful protector and showed her a lot of love and attention. He was the best father and helped in every way. He told her the truth in love when she was wrong.

Mary found a checker at the base grocery store who wouldn't charge her for all the food she was buying. She always got in his line. She also found a man at a good beauty shop in the mall that would never let her pay. It was his way of protesting the war. Mary's moral compass was broken.

Dennis, on the other hand was in line at the bank to cash his monthly check and the teller gave him $100 extra. Mary started thinking what they could do with an extra $100 when she noticed Dennis drove around again and got back in the line to hand it back. Nothing wrong with his moral compass!

Every day Mary watched the Watergate Hearings. Trust in government crumbled. She could trust the words of rock and roll and country singers more than politicians. It was the end of life as Mary knew it. Trust, honor and true statesmen were missing. When Nixon boarded his plane for home and held up two fingers, Mary held up one of her own.

Behind the curtain, the rancorous battle for Mary's soul and life continued. Demon forces worked on her distrust of everything and thought they had her right where they wanted her. They could not understand what the angel saw in her. The angel did not know either, but was confident in his orders. The Unseen Voice was counting down, self- assured in His plan for Mary. Timing was everything!

THE UNSEEN POWER

Finally, the day came when Dennis' service to his country was over. The moving van came, packed them up, and Mary put baby in his unsafe car seat. They drove to the base one more time to get Dennis' last pay, and started the long drive back to Denver. Dennis was happy, and Mary was pregnant again.

Since graduating from high school and starting work, Mary had saved $12,000. She had the gift of saving. No credit cards, live with what you have, and never pay interest. It was like throwing money away.

They had enough for a down payment on a little three-bedroom home in the area Mary grew up in. Life was good. Dennis started his job back at Ford where they added two years to his length of service. They were a wonderful company that took care of their employees. Mary was guaranteed this birth was not going to be done by the Army Regulations!

On March 23, 1975, Mary went into labor about 9:30 p.m. She was cutting Dennis' hair and watching Columbo on television. Again, Mary felt impelled to take a warm bath. Dennis was in a hurry to get her to the hospital this time. They wheeled her into the labor room at 10:30 p.m. and she was the first one out of the delivery room, 11:55. Her obstetrician barely made it to the hospital.

There was a problem. This baby was sunny side up, and labor pains were in her back and legs. Lamaze had no effect. The doctor wanted to knock her out and turn the baby over. Again, she heard the The Unseen Voice, "No!" She had learned to listen. Mary yelled, "No! Don't touch me! I will get this baby out myself!" Dennis was in the room but did not argue with Mary.

Shocked, the doctor backed up and sat down on a stool. Safely and quickly Mary pushed her baby out. Now they had two beautiful sons. Natural birth again this time.

This delightful baby had reddish hair. He stopped fussing every time they handed him to Mary. He knew his mama. Mary could see he had the gift of joy. Mary recovered quicker this time and home by the third day.

They found out later her doctor had been drinking that night. During another late-night delivery he killed a baby by breaking his skull turning him over like he wanted to do with Mary's baby. The Unseen Voice saved Mary's son's life.

This little baby was so content he slept through the night. He crawled like babies were supposed to. He nursed until he was a year old. He did not walk until he was 13 months and he smiled at everybody. What a joy! He was definitely going to be a people person!

Mary loved her two boys. They both had the gift of running like gazelles with super stamina. They both ran the Governor's 10K race through downtown Denver They ran the Boulder-Boulder, and other 5 and 10K races. They always finished getting a medal in their age bracket. They were beautiful to watch!

The older son turned out to be a lot like Dennis, protective, strong in Spirit, and hard working. The younger son was a lot like Mary, with the gift of compassion, and love for all people.

One afternoon, a neighbor across the street, Reenie, walked into Mary's lonely world and invited her to a Bible study. They offered free babysitting and a gourmet lunch. An afternoon with someone watching the boys and a chance to talk to adults. Mary was in.

Around the table were twelve women of different ages. The guest speaker looked them all over, then pointed her finger at Mary. "Are you going to Heaven?"

"Well, I don't know."

"If you don't know, you're not going!"

Mary wondered if had made a mistake. She had only been in the house 15 minutes, called out and told she was not going to Heaven. She was offended, but heard The Unseen Voice say "Sometimes God offends the mind to stir the heart."

The lady went on to talk about how Jesus came into her life and how angels bought her pigs when she was out of money; and how her sow backed up to the fence to give birth, so she could help but didn't have to get into the pen. She was afraid of the pigs.

Another lady told about her experience with Jesus, how He kept her from a bad marriage. Another woman, Mary's age, told how Jesus had saved her life after a terrible boating accident. Thrown from the boat, the propeller cut her head open. Her brains were exposed and they gave her no chance to live.

Something in Mary started to stir. How could this lady know she was absolutely going to Heaven while Mary was not? Were these women talking about The Unseen Voice?

Mary knew that there were things in this world nobody could see or explain. No matter how invisible she was to her family, she had been connected to an eternal spiritual realm. By whom and for what was always the question.

Mary still felt offended, but also jealous that these women had something she did not—absolute faith. They were friends of His, someone Unseen who could help them bear their loads in a personal way.

The next week was even more interesting. An elderly lady had prayed for a tape recorder to listen to sermons because she could not go to church. A man she did not know came to her door and handed her a new tape recorder.

Another woman was in a terrible dust storm in Boulder as she drove up a mountain. Her car twisted sideways. A man walked out of the storm, pushed her car back onto the road, never said a word, and walked back into the storm. She knew it was God who saved her life.

Mary began to believe these women were talking about a vital living relationship with Jesus Christ. It was different from the list of sins the church lady expounded. This was something alive!

On the way home, Mary looked up to the sky and thought, "*If you are real, you are going to have to show me. I cannot believe by just hearing other people's experiences. Who are you?*" He had been showing her Himself all her life, but she asked for more.

The next Sunday was Mother's Day, 1975. Mary woke up very early because her two-year-old was crying.

Mary laid in bed, furious at Dennis. It was Mother's Day, for crying out loud. Couldn't Dennis let her sleep in on Mother's Day? Baby cried louder and louder while Dennis slept deeper and deeper.

Mary walked into her son's room with frustration, darkness, and extreme guilt for the way she felt. Everything she had hoped for was coming true except within herself--who she had become. No blaming her family now. They were out of the picture.

The Unseen Voice became an Unseen Power and gently pushed her to the floor. He held her down and completely covered her. Her instinct was to struggle against this Power. She no longer heard her baby crying.

The Unseen Voice told her over and over, "I love you." Warm sweet honey flowed down her body into her soul changing her entire being. She relaxed to listen. Don't fight against something so soothing.

"*He maketh me lie down in green pastures.*" To get through to her, He had to hold her down to make her stop long enough to receive His love.

Maybe He had come to the wrong house. With her cursing addiction and bad moral compass, how could He love her? Didn't He see her heart? Nothing worth redeeming there!

He did not listen to her thoughts. He waited for her to be still and know He is Lord.

He stroked her hair and filled her with a love purer than anything she could ever imagined. She never wanted to leave this floor. It felt pure, white, shiny sparkling gold, and a soothing salve to calm all her screaming wounds and scars.

After some time passed, she again started to resist. She explained she could never be good enough to be a Christian. She was trying to be as truthful possible.

He repeated, "I love you, and you are Mine. You have been loosely on my vine since I created you in your mother's womb. You have always belonged to me. I know everything about you. I see you! I have sat in your grave."

She was not invisible to Him. He knew everything about her and saw her inside and out. She knew He was The Unseen Voice who had always been there.

"Okay, but I'm not going to church or ever read the Bible. I'm not that kind of person. I've tried but I just don't understand it."

Mary did not like women who were Christians. They all seemed blindly optimistic, self-driven, focused on things that could help them like finding a parking place. They did not live in reality. Mary was realistic, and knew this world was not a good place to live.

She ended up saying, "As much as I would like to, I do not believe I can do this."

The Unseen Voice said, "Yes, you are right. You cannot do it. I will do it for you if you let Me in." Mary said, "How do I do that?" She was used to controlling her own destiny.

He said five words: "***Get up and follow Me.***"

Mary's resistance was gone. "You are my Warrior, Mary. All things are new from this point on." She felt an excitement she never had before. She did have a purpose!

He released her to go any way she decided. She was free. She had no idea how long she was down on the floor. Time had no meaning. When she stood up, she knew two things were absolute. First, Jesus was real and was The Unseen Voice. Second, she would never be the same again. She had been changed by His hand. He had touched her.

When she walked into her son's room, Mary was full of darkness, anger and guilt. When she walked out of his room, she was full of light, love and joy, totally seen and spoken to by the Almighty God.

She returned to her bedroom and looked at her sleeping husband. "Thank you, God. He didn't wake up first today, on this Mother's Day morning." Maybe God put him in a deep sleep. Mary's depression left and she experienced for the first time what it felt like not to be clinically depressed. She felt so light she could fly. All her worries had disappeared. She knew He was always there.

The load she carried on her shoulders trying to have a perfect family with two babies and a husband were released from her. With a loud clunk, the chains of this world came off and fell on the ground. She heard them hit the floor. Without knowing it, she had been a slave. Now she stood up, free.

She thought she had been independent, but she wasn't. The devil worked on her and her family. Along the way, the Unseen Voice would not lose her before her time came. This second was her time! She grew up silent, but this Warrior thing would be much different.

No longer speaking in profane language or afraid to speak, but His way. Mary had a lot to learn!

She knew by the way He answered her prayer, she was definitely His favorite, just like she was her grandpa's favorite. This was a special calling. Heaven touched earth in her son's bedroom on Mother's Day, 1975. God picked her up off the desert floor, parched and dirty, cleaned her up and gave her a purpose. She would never doubt His love.

Mary asked The Lord the number one question she had all of her life, "Why did You give me the family that caused me so much pain?"

"I gave you the family I wanted you to have."

Mary seemed to understand. That was good enough for now. She knew she would know more along the way. Some things are good *to* you and some things are good *for* you. This was part of His plan preparing Mary for the purpose He created her for. It was not going to be the best of Mary and the best of God, it would be the "brokenness of Mary" and the "perfectness of God."

Mary realized God did not remove suffering, He shared it with her. He was creating in her something of great worth—courage and power. He was helping Mary grow strong, to be His Warrior. She had to do this alone.

For the first time she felt God's love for her family. She was to honor them and gently lead them to God's love no matter what.

Mary could not picture Dennis ever becoming a Christian to believe in a God he could not see. But she had more love to give him than he would ever know. She accepted being one of those women with an unsaved husband and did not even pray for him. God would have His way with Dennis like He did with her. Her love for him would see them through.

Mary's life was divided in two by the mighty sword of God: owning all control to relinquishing all control; never liking anybody to loving everybody; walking in darkness and death to walking in light and life; worry and peace. All things were indeed new.

Her eyes were opened to things she had never imagined. She saw people standing in line to pay for their prescriptions that needed Mary's financial help. She saw people at a gas station that needed to be told "God loves you." She made it a practice to give away at least $50 a month when God showed their need. She bought a newly released prisoner new shoes because he had no money and was walking in slippers. Giving gave Mary so much joy. She was no longer a slave to saving, but used what God gave her to help others.

People would walk up to Mary in grocery stores she had never seen before and tell her their mother was dying.

Mary would pray with them. Her light was shining!

She took her boys on bus rides. They walked up to strangers on the bus and said, "I think you dropped this," then gave them a five-dollar bill for lunch. Mary wanted her boys to be givers.

Mary also knew the devil was real. It was as if God pulled back a curtain for her to see God and the devil working. She saw God in some people and the devil in others. Her life started to make sense. The serial killers, thieves, murderers, accidents, and death, were Satan's workers, the devil's slaves. She saw demons in people's houses or on them. Other people were God's work. He wanted them to wake up, get up, start moving, follow Him, not their own worldly desires.

With her discernment, a young woman approached her for money to be able to drive home to get back to her baby. Mary said "I'll meet you across the street and put gas in your van." When she was done a young man, who had been hiding, stuck his head out the door and said, "God Bless You." Mary said, "God blesses me whether I put gas in your car or not. Why don't you live your life in such a way that God can bless you?" She told him that he needed to say, "Thank you." His lifestyle did not have the power to be handing out God's blessings

Mary was right in the second grade when she asked her teacher about people looking out of their own eyes and seeing different things. Demons and angels were certainly different!

Mary realized rheumatic fever gave her a compassion for people with problems. She could walk into a room and head straight for the person with the biggest problem. God had been teaching her eternal things. He gave her the gift of compassion.

She was definitely in a tug-of-war between Heaven and hell. Heaven had always won and God kept her from dying young. He was her unseen umbilical cord pumping into her what she needed when she needed it!

Who could resist a love so pure, uncontaminated, so perfect? She had no idea where that would take her or what she could do for Him. But whatever it was, she was going to do it with all her heart. No questions asked. No hesitation. She decided to start walking and He would show her what to do.

First baby step: she walked to the mall and ended up in a bookstore in front of The Living Bible. She bought it.

She started in Matthew not knowing what she would find.

Mary found herself. Poor in Spirit, mourning, meek, hungry, thirsty for righteousness, lost, weary and heavy- laden.

She also found Jesus, the Father and the Holy Spirit. Forgiving, loving His enemies, "Come to me all you who are weary and heavy laden, and I will give you rest."

Giving Mary rest was definitely Jesus. Turning the other cheek to those who hated Him? Jesus. He died with dirty feet so Mary's could be clean.

"He has chosen you because our gospel came to you not simply with words but also with power (holding Mary down on the bedroom floor), with the Holy Spirit (pouring out love) and with deep conviction (knowing at that very second in time her life had changed 180 degrees)."

The Truth was a Power much stronger than anything else. "Nothing could separate Mary from the love of God. "Not death or life, not angels or demons, not things in the present or things in the future, not even the powers of hell, height or depth, could separate her from the love of God." Mary could hear a ring of a bell when truth was spoken.

God's love is the most powerful thing in the Universe and He poured it out on Mary. Thankfulness was an understatement. She felt bound to Him forever no matter what happened. A Warrior needed a horse, but Mary didn't feel as if she could ask Him for anything. If He never did another thing for her again, He had done enough already. Joy was overflowing.

Mary could not put the Bible down. The more she read, the more she hungered to know Him more intimately. On every page she saw character traits of God. He was love, grace, mercy and justice.

Mary read her Bible for hours every day while watching her kids play or taking a nap. She was blown away by how meticulous God was, listing every name, measuring every cubit, mentioning lice and mustard seeds almost too small to see. Stars and planets so far away. Everything to help His creation live a long, wonderful life--air to breathe, beauty to enjoy, snow to melt to water the plants.

And did he have some creative punishments for the hard-hearted. Everything was so perfect! She read it straight through three times.

Mary would pray as she read, "Lord help me be like Abraham, full of faith; and not selfish like Lot."

"Help me be like Hannah and not like Peninnah, giving Hannah such grief for not being able to have children." "Please forgive me for the way I treated my sister."

"You spoke to Samuel when he was just a boy! You spoke to me at four years old!" "Help me be like David and not like Saul."

She filled up her notebook, to find out who she was, who Jesus was and wanted her to be for His eternal purpose.

Reading that Bible became Mary's prayer.

She felt like she was in communication with Him all the time without a special time for prayer. She always looked up to talk to Him, never down with her eyes closed. She never let him out of her thoughts. He was always speaking to her, turning her, changing her mind. If something came up, Mary sat with God and stopped, looked and listened. Sometimes He was specific, sometimes He would say, "I don't care."

She went back to the bookstore and bought many more Living Bibles to give away to people like her who needed to know who God really was.

She went over to her best friend of many years. She was leaving her husband for a man at work, breaking up her marriage and his. She ran in a circle of other women doing the same thing. Mary knew their relationship was over. She gave her a Bible and watched her put it on the shelf to gather dust. Fifteen years later when her husband left her for a younger woman, she picked it up. All things became new.

One day the vet came to her house to check on Mary's Boxer, Abby. They started a conversation and he said, "I can't believe in a God who made hell for people who would not believe in Him. That sounds so egotistical."

Mary, came right back with, "You've got it all wrong. God created hell for Satan. He also created Heaven. Satan deserves hell and he is down here trying to get people to follow him. God's will is that no person ever follows Satan to hell. God would never force us. He gave us all a choice, and freedom. We can use that choice to follow Satan and end up with him, or follow God and end up where we were always supposed to be."

The vet was astounded. The lie Satan led him to believe was exposed! He had never thought of it that way. He thanked Mary and would not charge her for coming to check on Abby. Mary had no idea she would say those words. They came off her lips like butter.

One little lie from the devil believed, separates us from our Creator.

While washing the dishes, Jesus said, "Submit to your husband. He is the man I have given you. A marriage will not survive with two heads. You have two different stations. One is not better than the other."

Dennis came into the kitchen with a bill from the doctor who had been drinking and did nothing to deliver their second son. She knew the doctor had to accept whatever Blue Cross paid him. She did not argue the point with Dennis because of what The Unseen Voice had just said. She sat down, wrote out a check and drove to the post office so she could not change her mind. It was key that Mary obeyed Jesus and showed the devil she was not going to worship money, even if she knew she was right and Dennis was wrong.

Mary knew God was working on Dennis. Everything was a battle of life or death. Every decision was intentionally checking her motives. She learned a lot about herself by doing that.

Two weeks later, the doctor sent the check back and told them to go out and have a nice dinner. That amount was groceries for three months. Jesus said, "If you submit, even the wrong things Dennis does, I will make turn out right."

Mary knew Jesus loved Dennis and her children. She was attending the School of the Holy Spirit of Warriors and determined to pass with straight A's.

She had always stayed in close touch with her grandma. The post office never canceled the stamp on Grandma's letters. Mary carefully peeled the stamps off and put them on her own envelopes to send a letter back to her grandma. She never thought about what she was doing.

She bought her own stamps and stopped peeling off Grandma's. She understood that everything she did was either making the devil happy or the Lord happy. There was no in-between. If she blew it like all the people in the Bible, she would turn to the Lord, ask His forgiveness and His help to do better. He promised He would forgive her and cleanse her. He made it clear she could not do this alone as she had done everything else. The Holy Spirit told Mary when she did wrong and was slowly repairing her cracked moral compass.

Mary came out of a store and saw three of the most beautiful candles on the bottom rack of a shopping cart next to her car. Mary could picture them on her dining room table and how they would light up the room. They were exactly the right color. She knew they were expensive. Her mind was in turmoil. She realized she could no longer act on her blind instinct. It was flawed. She had to be intentional about every choice she made. This was going to be hard. Temptation was knocking at the door.

She took the candles back into the store and said, "Somebody forgot to take these out of their basket in the parking lot." Her moral compass was being repaired. She laughed as she walked back to her car. She thought it was no accident they were candles and Mary did not hide her light under a basket.

Dennis found wallets and cell phones and always returned them to their rightful owner never accepting a reward. God used Dennis to keep others from stealing and he didn't even know it. His moral compass was always true north.

God showed Mary in a profound way why He had to die on the cross to save those who followed Him. She partook in His suffering during his death and it changed her. His cross became personal to her. When a man dies, it is one thing. When Jesus, the Son of God dies, it is something else.

Mary did not fit in with Christian ladies. One made a big deal about how God helped her pick between two tablecloths. Another lady told Mary if she did not buy whole wheat bread, she could not see how Mary was a Christian.

Mary soon learned about these wacko Christians out there with crazy ideas. She believed God was building His Kingdom. He asked people to do what they were created for, loving Him and loving everybody else with His love. If you say you believe but don't get up and follow Him, doing what he asks for His eternal glory, your belief is nil and void. Faith isn't about what to eat or what tablecloth you buy.

Mary did something unusual with Dennis. She kept her mouth shut for months. She never told him anything about her new-found faith or what had happened on Mother's Day. She could not prove it so it would only drive Dennis farther away. He noticed something different in her, but thought the ladies in the Bible study were having a good influence.

Three months later, Reenie and Mary thought it would be good for Dennis to meet Reenie's husband Jim, who was a pastor. Mary invited them for dinner. Dennis had questions for Pastor Jim: "How do you pastor a church?" "Why do you spend so much time at home?" "How has your life changed?" "How do you get paid?"

Pastor Jim told Dennis stories about his life, how he became a Christian at KU, then transferred to UCLA. He was on the beach one day, when Bill Bright invited him for breakfast. Bill Bright had started Campus Crusades for Christ and Jim thought he could get a free breakfast out of it so he went. Bill told Pastor Jim about what he was doing, then left the bill for Jim to pay. It hit Jim that God knew what had been in his heart. That changed Jim. He had became a follower of Christ. He shared story after story of hearing from God and getting up and doing it. Jim and Reenie were walking Warriors.

Pastor Jim had a way of speaking truth and was not afraid to share his personal failures. In all of Denver, Dennis and Mary could not have lived by a better couple to watch and learn. Jim and Reenie had been doing for years what God told Mary to do, *"Get up and follow Me."*

After dinner Pastor Jim thanked Mary and went home.

Mary asked Dennis, "Do you want to know how all of this has affected me?" "No." His answer did not surprise her.

Two nights later Dennis woke her up at two in the morning and said, "I told Jesus if You are real and will get involved with my life like you did Jim's, I will give you my life. I actually felt Him come into my Spirit."

Mary made him repeat what he had said because he had been crying for hours and having difficulty speaking. He added, "Since 10 o'clock last night, I have been trying to tell you. But something had a hold of my throat and I couldn't speak until now."

Mary knew exactly what had a hold of his throat. They were in a battle and the devil did not want to lose another one who he convinced could not know God if he could not see him. "If you confess with your mouth Jesus is Lord and believe in your heart that God raised Him from the dead, you will be saved...it is with your mouth that you confess and are saved." Romans 10:9

Saved from God's judgment of people who chose to believe a lie of the devil. Saved from being broken, living in a broken world with broken people. Saved from what the devil ruined. God stepped in to make all things new and give His creation another chance.

Dennis had a spiritual fight to confess with his mouth, but he won. Mary was astonished. Now the two of them could follow Christ together! The next morning was Sunday and Dennis wanted to go to Pastor Jim's church. Jim invited Dennis to tell everyone what happened to him. Even though Dennis was shy, he told strangers how Jesus became a living Spirit to him! The church started singing Proverbs 3:5 "Trust in the Lord with all your heart and lean not on your own understanding. In all your ways acknowledge Him and he will direct your paths."

That hit Dennis like being plunked on the head with a yardstick. He did not need to understand it all right now. He needed to trust God and follow.

Mary knew they were going to have a real marriage, a covenant between them and God. Carrying a Bible down the aisle on her wedding day made sense to her now. God's Word would be in the center of their marriage.

The next Sunday the church was going to have a baptism at someone's swimming pool. Mary did not expect Dennis to go because of his Catholic roots. He looked at her and said, "Let's go!" They hurried home after church, got into their swim suits and went to be baptized.

From that moment on, things started happening to Dennis. He looked for the number at work where he could order light bulbs. The phone suddenly rang and a voice said, "Dennis, do you need any light bulbs?" He had been gone over two years.

Dennis wanted to find his little pocket Bible given to him when he enlisted in the Army. He had not seen it for ages. He sat on the sofa put his hand down into the cushion and pulled it up. They did not even own that sofa when he lost it.

God does not always work this way, but He was building their faith to use their gifts for His earthly Kingdom.

Two weeks after Mother's Day, Mary heard someone curse. It struck her as something the enemy relished. She could hear his delight. Demons have a sound, God has a sound, and truth has a sound. She was familiar with all three. She realized God had completely taken that addiction away from her. What was a big problem for her was no big problem for God. Now, she had to learn to speak the truth in love.

Dennis was worried about his father. Praying as he mowed the grass, God gave him a scripture out of the blue, exactly where it was and what it said. Dennis knew nothing about the Bible, but he was determined. He put his Bible under his arm and went to his Dad's apartment. A few days later, his Dad gave his life to Jesus.

Dennis was convicted by the Holy Spirit that he held on too tightly to his coin collection. It had become an idol.

He would not let Mary touch it. He sold it for $400.

Mary thought, *"Great! Our refrigerator is about ready to go out and that would buy a new one."* Dennis had another idea. He took the $400 to their Friday night Bible Study and put it in the basket for the man who was taught the lessons. Dennis exchanged his idol for the Word of God.

From that day on, God mightily blessed them financially. Dennis was never a lover of money and brought the blessings of the Lord into their home. Mary was so happy to be married to a man like this. As far as the refrigerator Mary wanted to use the money for, things worked out and they were never in need.

Mary had a vision that she, her mother and sister were sitting at Mary's kitchen table. A light came down on her mother and sister. Mary knew they would become Christians, too.

Mary's sister and two children lived with them while her husband was stationed in Thailand. Dennis told her, "I want you to know that I forgive you for everything you did."

She could not see how Dennis could forgive her for the way she acted towards him and Mary, but this gave her relief. When she came to live with them, she started following Christ. She saw the change in Mary and Dennis and felt their love. She had heard the Unseen Voice speak to her many times and He always called her by her first and middle name.

As soon as she decided to Follow Christ, her husband was miraculously transferred to the Philippines where the family could go. She grew by watching Christian TV and helping Nuns with their projects.

Seven years later their family came to live with Mary's family for a month while they were waiting for his new assignment. They had come many times. Mary had prayed when they visited for her sister's husband to come to Christ. Nothing happened. This time she told God, "I'm not praying for him. It is useless."

The Unseen Voice said, "Mary, what if you gave up one time too soon?" It gave her hope that God was not finished with her brother-in-law.

At Mary's house, he was bored not in the air flying fighter jets. He sat in her family room surrounded by the mundane things of life. Mary threw him a Bible from the kitchen and said, "Here, read this. Start from the beginning."

He was astonished God would tell His army to kill men, women and children. That was not what he knew about God. He asked Mary why.

"Because that's what we all deserve. But Jesus took our death for us if we believe and follow Him." He kept reading. One night another fighter pilot friend asked them out to dinner.

When they returned, Priscilla said, "You will never believe what happened! His friend talked all night about how they had become Christians." God was answering prayers.

His new assignment was at the War College in Alabama. The base commander said at introductions, "You will be at my Bible Study every Tuesday night, won't you?"

"Yes, sir!"

A few weeks later he called Dennis. "Would you fly here and baptize me? I can rent the YMCA pool for 15 minutes so you can baptize me and my children. I became a Christian while I was jogging last week. I don't want to be baptized into a church, I want to be baptized into Christ. No one knows this yet."

Mary's whole family traveled to Alabama for the baptism. Later, they all had communion together. The fabric of Mary's family was changing! For years, Mary's brother-in-law who made General, has taught Bible studies to other cadets and officers who respected him. How far around the world has this man sent God's Word?

Filling Empty Spaces

The Lord gave Mary exceptional people to teach her what she was lacking. Natalie was the most nurturing woman in all of Denver, maybe the whole earth. She hugged Mary a lot and showed her how delighted she was in her. Natalie saw what God put in Mary. She saw Mary's soul. She also taught her how to nurture her boys.

She made Mary feel so good, not in a fleshly or prideful way, but reinforced the Spirit of God in her. Mary could tell Natalie anything and Natalie would say, "Well, that's wonderful!" She was interested in Mary's faith and always wanted to know more. Mary was changing as Natalie nurtured her God's way. She taught Mary to not flatter people, but to see who they were in their hearts and comment on that.

Natalie was God's true blessing with heaps of laughing and hugging. Just what that little girl in Mary needed. Natalie had the gift of hospitality and her love overflowed. No matter when Mary showed up, she was just the person Natalie wanted to see. She had so many comfortable chairs in her living room Mary felt at home.

Natalie was a baker and always had something to serve. She offered a mug and bowl club for her neighborhood.

Everyone brought their own mugs and bowls for hot soups and delicious drinks.

The second friend God gave Mary was Ella. She was a strong woman God used mightily. She was in the first Bible study Mary went to with Rcenie.

Ella helped Mary know for sure she could be a genuine Christian and not have to change her personality to be like Christians Mary had trouble with. Ella was not a typical Christian. Mary knew she would not be either. Ella was a Warrior and she and Mary shared the gift of discernment.

Discernment had to be handled carefully. If used correctly, the Christian will not have many friends. People don't like to hear truth about themselves, but if they won't listen to God, He will use someone else to tell them. The person with discernment becomes an enemy. Ella taught Mary that she stood before an audience of One, her Maker.

Mary had the problem of working so hard to get her family to love her. She had to let it go. God's love had to be enough.

God showed Mary things no one else would see, such as demons. Mary could see them hanging onto people as they sped past on their motorcycles. She once went to a Bible study and saw the word "Witchcraft" over one of the ladies. As the evening went on, this lady shared how she was a witch and still used some of the powers. Mary knew before she even opened her mouth.

Mary could always tell the difference between a "religious spirit" and a true relationship with God. She did not know how, but she knew immediately.

Mary always noticed how people's prayers were "me-centered". Mary did not pray for traveling mercies because she believed God was sending her. He would take care of her. He could heal her if He wanted to, so she left that up to Him.

It was a walk of faith learning to pray for what He wanted her to do each day, each hour, each minute. Stop, look, and listen. Let Him into your thoughts and desires. Move intentionally and carefully. Mary was His vessel He was molding and He would take care of her.

God showed Mary the souls of people. She knew if a believer was standing in front of her. Mary often told people, "You are a Christian" before striking up a conversation.

One man said, "Well, yes, I am." He showed Mary pictures of his brothers and sisters who were also Christians and thanked her for knowing his faith showed!

Mary told one man who was complaining about having no money, "You would if you stopped going to strip clubs and drinking." She had no personal knowledge he did this, but he said. "Yes, you are exactly right."

Another man stepped into an elevator at a hospital Mary had pushed the down button. He pushed up. When it started going down, he said, "That is just like my life. When I try to go up, I always go down." Mary said, "No, that is just like Jesus. He had to go down before we could go up." The man looked at her and thanked her for reminding him of that and said, "You just made my day!"

Once Mary was at someone's house and a demon followed her home. It started shaking the bed. Mary rolled over and went to sleep. It never came back.

Mary had learned two things. Never fear death and never fear demons or Satan. Not fearing takes their power away. Fearing them makes them stronger.

With the gift of discernment, Mary saw many things she did not want to see. The world looked more dangerous and disgusting. God chooses which gifts He gives and He always said, "Be strong, Mary. Be strong."

If Ella listened to a sermon, and thought it was not right, she would say, "That's a bunch of crap." She taught Mary how to be herself because Ella was herself and never apologized for it. Ella never argued with people but would speak the truth and let them that hear, hear.

When she spoke of people in the Bible, she made them out to be real people, not caricatures. Peter was depressed, Paul was sick, Thomas wanted to believe but had trouble getting there, Jesus was tired. Ella said what the Bible said, not what people wanted to make it say.

She taught Mary by being an example. Ella showed Mary how God gave them their personalities for a reason. If Mary saw something that did not line up with scriptures, it was her job to speak it out. "Tell it like it is," she would say.

God does not want us to think about our bodies more than we think about Him--what we eat, what we wear, how we feel. Mary lived in severe pain most of her adult life but still kept her eyes foremost on Jesus. His grace was enough. She was bold handling the pain.

Mary went off by herself and learned from the Holy Spirit before she ever started going to church and listening to other people's ideas. She learned how to put the Old Testament together with the New Testament. Mary learned God does not change. Twisting the scriptures always happens to attract people (and their money). Mary and Ella believed they should stick to following the Lord in the same direction! Twists and turns were never right. He is the same yesterday, today and forever.

Ella had a lot of money she was always willing to share. She taught Mary having money was not good or bad, it just was what it was.

Mary lost track of Ella, but a phone call from Reenie told her Ella was dying in Florida. Mary called and Ella said, "I was just telling Bob last week, "I really like that Mary." She was not afraid to tell it like it is." No, Mary was not afraid.

Forty years later on her death bed Ella was still mentoring Mary. She showed Mary what a Warrior was. Even if she got hurt, God would always pick her back up. Her shell on the outside was getting harder, while Mary's heart got softer. Mary would never have been who she was without Ella, Natalie and Reenie as she began her journey.

Reenie taught Mary how to drop everything and follow Him by her example. Mary and Reenie became good friends as Christians, mothers, and neighbors. Reenie was from California and introduced Mary to foods she had never heard of: avocados, eggplant, artichokes, and sprouts. They both had grape vines. When it was harvest time, they put their grapes together to can in mason jars, like Mary's grandma did. Their jam tasted much better using both kinds of grapes than just one. The grapes always made Mary think of how God wants us to be together with other Christians to produce better fruit while attached to his vine!

One day Mary walked out of a hospital visit and got lost in the massive structure. A nurse came up to her and asked, "Can I help you?"

"I'm lost and don't know how to get back to my car." "Be careful what you say, you are hung by your tongue."

"I am not hung by anything, I serve a God who thinks I am His favorite." Mary found her car.

As a chaplain, Mary gave a man Last Rites. That morning, Mary was at another company and a Catholic lady offered her three Catholic books. One of them was a book of beautiful Catholic prayers, which included Last Rites.

Thirty minutes later Mary received the request from the man's family. Mary offered to try and find a priest, but they declined. None of them had been to church in a long time and the man was dying quickly. Mary knew in her heart God was going ahead of her by giving her the book.

She drove to the hospital, and found the man and sister in ICU. She connected with his mother on the phone, opened up the book and read out the parts she could agree with as a prayer for this dying son.

Mary felt God wanted her to give the mother some peace. Receiving the Catholic Prayer Book that morning was His miracle. Mary made the cross on his forehead with oil. He died a couple of hours later with a mother and sister who had been comforted.

God gave Mary many visions and dreams to show her His ways. She saw how demons dropped people when they were through with them. She saw some murders committed and exactly what was said and how it happened. She had one dream that she was with a pastor looking through the sheep and they were sick, but they could not find out where. They looked fine. That dream God repeated to her twice and told her, "I've given it to you twice, now don't forget it." In 1978, Mary had a dream she was walking down a street in New York City, looked through the buildings and saw a large airplane flying low. It flew into a building she could not see, blocked by other buildings. She ran towards it, but people started walking toward her covered with white ash. One black lady looked very disoriented with white ash all over her body, especially on her face. Mary ran up to her, took her by the shoulders and said, "Jesus saved you! Jesus saved you!" Mary hugged her.

On 9/11, Mary watched television as her dream unfolded. She was glued to the set as the buildings fell and that same disoriented lady from her dream walked right toward the camera.

Maybe Mary will learn more about this later. God is never rushed to reveal what He is trying to show us. But Mary knows there was some reason.

Mary started typing legal transcripts out of her home. During a national union meeting, Mary's boss talked about going into a hotel room with his dog. The hair on the back of his dog's neck stood straight up and he would not move.

Her boss asked, "Do you believe there are things out there we can't see?" "Absolutely."

"What do you think they are?"

Mary knew he wanted her to say ghosts or dead people, but she took a deep breath and said, "Demons or angels."

"I don't believe in that stuff. I believe in reincarnation. God is going to let me come back and do it better next time."

"Why would He do that when He's giving you a chance to do better right now? The Bible says you die once then the judgment. Get up and follow Him now. Sorry, this is all you get."

He was not happy Mary challenged him. But Mary's purpose was to follow Him, not type tapes.

Mary was learning. She had avoided confrontations all her life. God was using her to take a deep breath and confront. If she did not do it, who would? Maybe nobody. Her boss always teased her about going to the Church of the Ding Dongs. This let Mary know he was still thinking about it.

One Sunday in church, Mary saw the Pastor (not Jim) look at the piano player. *"Oh no! They were having an affair."*

No proof, just the way they looked at each other. It was so strong Mary went to the pastor and said, "I thought you loved us more than that."

"More than what?" "You know."

He turned around and walked off. Yes, he knew. The piano player's husband had recently died. She was a beautiful young woman going through grief with young children. The Pastor's wife and children were not with him at the time.

The next Sunday he preached on the seven things God hates--"The worst is God hates people who spread discord among the brethren." He aimed the verbal arrow directly at Mary. Although Mary never talked about it, the devil made sure it was getting around to destroy Mary.

Mary decided to answer him back. "Did you know we cannot even eat with someone who calls himself a brother, and is a fornicator?" He walked off again.

Every night, Mary prayed, "Please God, take this idea away from me. Let me wake up tomorrow and it be gone." But it never left. It grew stronger. Mary loved this man of God and this truth was tearing her up.

Everyone in the church began to hate Mary. They thought she was being used by the devil to break up a good church. The Church was in a battle they did not know and could not see. This pastor was going to lead them astray. Sexual sin most always accompanies false doctrine. Mary learned you can't just hear what they say, you must watch carefully what they do.

The piano player called Mary and asked her to come over. She was on the verge of a nervous breakdown. The pastor told her to seek mental help because it only happened in her mind. He told her to stay away from Mary, because she was a tool of the devil.

"But look, Mary, he wrote me all these letters." She opened a box and Mary started reading. He said, "I have had *many* women, but none has satisfied me like you do." They were planning to take the church money and start a new life together.

Mary told her she had known about the affair for three months. "Bring the letters and come with me."

They met with the church elders, and the piano player told her story. The pastor proved his own sin by his written words.

As the elders read the letters, their eyes opened to the truth. Mary watched as scales fell off.

The pastor left town, but not with the piano player or the money. The situation harmed a lot of people who watched a good preacher fall and a young widow taken advantage of.

He went to California to start another church. Mary was the only one he wrote an apology letter to, probably because she called him out on it. Yes Mary, this new Christian to a seasoned 50-year-old third-generation pastor. He was dangerous to the flock.

Mary sat down and considered everything they were taught by this man. She built her faith around Jesus, the chief cornerstone. As hurt as she was, she considered this a vital teaching from the Lord. Test every teacher. God was going to use her for what He created her for. Mary learned to never be afraid to speak the truth no matter how high up in the church people are. Especially if they are high up in the church. Iron sharpens iron.

God gave Mary Jo, who was the truest of friends. Jo knew the Lord well and sat at His feet, sometimes just to keep going. Jo always had her back when Mary needed it. They've been friends over 40 years. They were always excited to talk about the Lord together.

They shared their ups and downs, always praying together in the midst of grave tragedies and heartbreak. They were tied together by the Lord with a cord that could not be broken. No matter where Mary moved, they were only a text or a phone call away. They took trips together and never stopped talking. Jo was the one true constant in Mary's life. When Mary would move, she never hung on to any of the friends she made. She moved to new and different people, except for Jo.

Mary and a friend started their own legal transcribing business in Denver typing court recordings out of their homes. Mary could make about $400 typing in the morning, then spend the rest of the day with her friends and boys.

It was interesting work and brought in quite a bit of money for Mary to invest in college funds for her boys and retirement. Mary's boys never went to day care, never came home to an empty house, were always picked up by their mother from school if they got sick, never wore shoes that were too tight, and always looked neat and clean. Mary had broken the dysfunctions of her family.

She leaned on the scripture, "Unless the Lord builds the house, they who labor, labor in vain." Mary knew to hold onto her business loosely and sold her 50% when she moved on.

From her business, Mary learned how to deal with bullies. This came in handy as a woman and a Christian. Some attorneys and bosses were bullies and tried to get what they wanted by yelling, cursing or lying.

In a nice voice, Mary said, "Now I know you have a wonderful education and a great vocabulary. When you can call me back and use that, please feel free to do so. Until then, your cassettes will be in my desk." Then she hung up. About a minute later they called back to apologize. Mary learned to stand up to people without getting mad—no matter who they were.

Through Mary's volunteer job once a week at Legal Aide in downtown Denver, Mary learned about mental illnesses, drug addiction and homelessness--issues she had never experienced herself, but God wanted her to see. She also learned how to put a case together that an attorney could take and run with it. God did not want Mary to stay in her safe neighborhood only knowing people like herself. He wanted to use her in a mighty way.

TRANSPLANTED AND PRUNED

The little steps started getting bigger. Mary and Dennis needed a larger house with a dining room and a garage. They bought a new build close to Columbine High School in Littleton. This was years before the school shootings of 1999. God had a way of putting them where they needed to be.

While their house was being built, Mary, Dennis and the boys stay at her parents' house for a month. They sold their little house for double what they paid for it.

One day as Mary typed in the dining room, Carol came in and watched. Carol said, "Mary, you are the fastest typist I have ever seen. You type much better than I."

It meant a great deal to Mary—this first compliment her mom had ever given her. Staying with Carol and Jim helped Mary's boys form a great relationship with their grandma and grandpa. They had a swimming pool in their back yard where they had great fun. Carol was a wonderful grandmother and truly loved all her grandchildren.

Mary, Dennis and the boys moved into their new house. Soon after, they volunteered with Young Life Ministry at Columbine High School. They knew many of the students. 200 kids met in the cafeteria to have fun, eat 100-foot banana splits, perform skits and hear about Jesus. Twice a year Mary and Dennis took the kids to Buena Vista, Colorado, to a beautiful Young Life Ranch.

Many students came to the Lord through the ministry of Young Life. Every Tuesday, Mary and Dennis had 30 students come to their house for Bible Study. Dennis taught the boys in the family room, while Mary taught the girls in the living room. Many of them had never heard the gospel. Students came to their house and asked "How can I be saved?" Construction workers knocked on their door to ask for prayer. Their house became a sanctuary.

One day, Mary drove up a hill close to their home. Several cars were stopped on the hill in front of her. More cars stacked up behind her. Tires squealed as a large dump-truck full of rocks crested the hill and barreled down from the other way.

Mary was trapped. The truck suddenly turned and pointed directly at her, approaching full force. Mary cried out, "Here I come, Lord!" and waited to die in the crash. She was ready.

But as the truck reached Mary's left side view mirror, it jerked and suddenly stopped. The Unseen Force was stronger than the dump-truck with no brakes racing down a steep hill full of rocks.

The driver climbed out. "My brakes gave out and I have no idea what made the truck turn toward you or what made it stop."

"I do," Mary said "demons made it turn towards me and angels made it stop."

The driver noticed a big scratch in Mary's side-view mirror. "May I replace that for you?" "No. I want to look at it every time I get in this van to remember what God did for me."

Mary figured this was the fourth time Jesus had saved her life. She knew she was a target and this battle was personal.

The story traveled around the county. Mary heard it several times from different people. Every telling was glory to God.

During the Denver winters, Mary often came down with pneumonia. One time she was too sick to go to the doctor. She laid in bed in pain trying to sleep and sensed the Lord in her bedroom. Her boxer dog jumped up and looked at Jesus.

Mary left the room with Jesus and He took her up to the cross. She thought she died. She felt good as long as she looked into the Lord's eyes.

"Look down," He said.

She saw hundreds of people, many she recognized. Some were family members. Others were groups of people full of hate and hypocrisy. Rich, poor, famous, all ages. They looked emaciated, dying of hunger, sick, the walking dead.

"I died for those people." "I know you did."

"Now you have to die for them, too."

Mary did not die of pneumonia that night, but she was taken to the cross and told to die to herself and live for these people so they could be free. Baby steps were over.

Seconds later, Mary was back in her bed. Jesus stood beside her and said, "Tell Dennis when he wakes up." The alarm rang almost immediately and Mary told him what had happened to her.

Dennis asked, "Do you feel condemnation about not having died for them?" "No, I felt there was no way I could die for them unless He helped me do it."

Throughout her life, the Lord worked on Mary to love more and give up worldly things she wanted. She must decrease so He could increase. No grudges. No prejudices. No fleshly judging allowed.

Dennis and Mary did many ministries and saw many miracles after that on the late-night back streets of Denver. They prayed with prostitutes, drug addicts and people going to porno movies. They would always ask, "Is there anything I can pray for you for?" It was amazing how many times the answer was, "Yes." They stopped suicides, brought people back to the Lord, and stopped drugs from having any effect. They would pray for two hours before they hit the streets and a lot of times, they knew who they were looking for.

After Thanksgiving, Mary's mother went to the hospital to have a blood clot in her leg checked. Mary was with her a few days later when the doctor came in and said, "Carol, you have lung cancer."

"How many years do I have?" "Not years, a few months."

Mary was devastated. Her mother was only 53, and the doctors could do nothing.

Mary wanted her mother and her boys to grow up having their grandmother who loved them. Mary's depression returned. Carol never asked why she had lung cancer. She knew it was from chain smoking. Mary helped Jim care for Carol and was with her most of the time.

Mary's old neighbor, Pastor Jim, saw Carol every day and read her Psalm 139. "O Lord, you have searched me and you know me. You hem me in—behind and before; you have laid your hand upon me. If I go up to Heaven, You are there. If I make my bed in the depths, You are there. Your hand will guide me, your right hand will hold me fast. How precious to me are your thoughts, O God!"

Carol listened, but she believed her sins of drinking, smoking and not going to church separated her from God.

There was no hope for her. Jim and Mary convinced her that was not true.

Everyone has sin, but nothing separates us from the love of God. Confess with your mouth and believe in your heart He is Lord.

One day close to her death Carol said, "I see it! These other religions know about God, but we can know God!

Whether He takes me today or lets me live ten more years, I put myself in His hands."

Mary knew she would see her mom again in Heaven. Carol finally saw God's love and felt His acceptance. In a second on her deathbed, she changed. Mary saw pure joy on her face.

Jim preached the funeral. It fulfilled the vision Mary had when two lights came down and illuminated her mother and sister at her kitchen table. They were both secure.

Mary felt no hope of having a full family who knew the Lord in this world. She was following Jesus, and had made an impact in eternal things, but she felt more and more alone.

Mary experienced how grief could hit you harder and stay longer than you ever realized possible. Mary was just 30 when her mom died. People said things that stung, but her friend Jo called and just cried with Mary. She was the only one Mary trusted with her grief.

Mary cried every day for six months! Dennis wondered when she was ever going to stop. He could do nothing.

Mary's heart was crushed. She needed her mom to be a mom.

Since Carol accepted Jesus right before she died, Mary did not get to have her as a Christian mom. She felt cheated. Her hopes for a different relationship were crushed.

The Lord didn't take the pain away, but He promised to be nearest the broken-hearted. The Unseen Voice said, "Lean into the pain and let it do its work. That was Carol's time to know Me."

To this day, Mary still needs a mom.

Within a month Mary's dad took off for Phoenix where he always wanted to live and play tennis year-round. He took a woman he knew from his country club. Mary felt as if she lost both her mom and dad.

Mary was a soccer mom, PTA president, room mother, while she ran her business.

She hugged her boys every day and told them how much she loved them. She was determined to be the mother she wished she would have had. Her oldest son's soccer team took a 21-day soccer tour through Europe. The whole family went. Mary did get to see Europe.

Dennis started on his Master's Degree. One day he came home from work devastated. He had been demoted because his boss wanted him to alter the books to make them look better. Dennis refused. His boss almost punched him then fired him. The depot manager gave him the only job open, security guard, checking workers' lunch pails as they left the building. His pay was cut. He looked for another job, but nothing opened up.

During this time, Mary sat at her kitchen table reading Isaiah. The Unseen Voice said, "In six months, you will be extremely surprised what I will do with Dennis."

Mary told Dennis what she heard. He quit looking for a job and worked every day with a smile on his face. Nobody knew the circumstances of his demotion. He would say nothing negative about his previous boss. He did not retaliate. Dennis earned the admiration and respect of the workers. He believed God was in control of demotions and promotions.

Men in the warehouse asked Dennis how he accepted this situation. He would tell them "This is in God's hands." A man asked, "Would you go to the hospital and pray for my mother?" He did.

In exactly six months, a position opened up as accountant in the front office, and it was given to Dennis. He was promoted again with another raise and ended up being his old boss's supervisor.

His old boss said, "I suppose you are going to fire me." Dennis said, "No, I'm not. I want you to be honest with the books, though. We can't fix what we don't know."

Before Dennis was transferred to Kansas City, his old boss came to him and said, "You were the best boss I ever had!" Workers actually cried to lose Dennis as their boss. God's blessing was on him.

A friend of the family was called Little Carol because she was named after Mary's mother. In her twenties she was pregnant but was also battling cancer. Mary was heart-broken, but visited her often. After a C-section delivery, they aggressively fought the cancer. Mary visited the NICU, rocked the baby and sang songs to her. Little Carol told the nurses Mary was her sister.

One night Mary invited all her friends to have a surprise baby shower for Little Carol's baby. The nurse brought the baby into Little Carol's room so she could dress her and hold her. It was a happy night for everyone, especially Little Carol.

Mary went to the hospital and saw her empty bed. The baby had gone home yesterday with her grandparents and Little Carol died.

Mary drove home with tears running down her face. She had a new appreciation for being alive, but grieved for this young woman Mary had known all her life.

Mary prayed, "Thank You, God, that I won't be helping dying people any more. It is just too hard on me." The Unseen Voice said, "There will be a lot more. You are not done."

Four years later at a water park, Mary saw Little Carol's baby girl. Mary told her how much her mother loved her. The little girl never let go of Mary's hand the whole time they were at the Park. Maybe she remembered the bond they shared in the NICU rocking and singing. God's gift to Mary.

The District Office at Ford was closing down in Denver. If Dennis wanted to stay with Ford, he would have to move his family to Kansas City. With the recession, jobs were scarce. They would move.

After 37 years in Denver, leaving was hard. Mary had so many friends she loved and loved her back. At her going-away luncheon fifteen women Mary had led to the Lord or mentored gave their testimonies. It was humbling to see them all together. Most of them did not know each other.

One young girl said, "Mary, I have a lot of friends who care about me, but you are the only one who cares about my soul." What better compliment than that!

Another one was dying the morning after Mary's mom had passed. She had no idea what grief Mary was experiencing. Her urethra was cut during surgery and she was poisoning herself quickly.

"Yes, I will come." Mary prayed for her.

"Wait, I feel something different!" God healed her.

A former pastor and his wife came to ask their forgiveness for teaching their church a false doctrine. He said during one sermon, "You can have anything you want from God if you believe." He looked and saw Mary's face wince. He came to ask them for forgiveness and tell them he repented and was going to a good seminary. Angels rejoice when people hear God and change.

Everyone had their own story at the luncheon. It was a good send-off.

Dennis, Mary and the boys moved into their new house in Kansas City during a heat wave. The temperatures spiked over 100 degrees during the day and only the 90's at night.

Kansas had the same smells and beauty as Iowa. It was extremely humid, hard for people from dry Denver to get used to. The trees were magnificent. You could actually see a true sunset because the mountains did not block the sun setting in the west.

Kansas City held the spirit of people who believed they were okay although they were not. Churches occupied every corner and were filled every Sunday. Parking places were hard to find. The people were not challenged to stop, look, and listen to Christ, to build His Kingdom. Going to Church was more of a tradition.

Dennis and Mary had a hard time finding a church that accurately taught scripture. Some taught only they could usher in the second coming of Christ. Mary walked out of churches in the middle of sermons. It was so disheartening.

Her gift of discernment was one gift that was not accepted. Some churches, Mary called one-gift churches, the gift of giving, the gift of prophecy, the gift of service. While these are all good gifts, Mary knew a healthy church would welcome all the gifts working together in harmony and not just focus on one and reject others. It was almost like a menu. If you like this, go to this church. If you like that, go to that church.

As Mary read the Bible, she noticed a pattern. Just before God did something great, he would tell the people to move.

Abraham left Ur

Jacob left his home

Joseph was sold into slavery and went to Egypt

David ran and hid in a cave from Saul

The Queen of Sheba left Ethiopia to visit Solomon

Moses fled to the desert for 40 years

Mary and Joseph went to Bethlehem

Wise men left Asia to follow a star

Shepherd boys left the sheep to find the baby born in Bethlehem

Mary and Joseph took Jesus to Egypt as a baby

Jesus went to the backside of the desert after he was baptized

The apostles left Jerusalem to take His Word to the world

All these leavings were for God's unseen reason. Mary felt better about leaving Denver. It was God's plan for them. If they stayed in the same place all their life they would not grow.

Mary felt like she was being pruned to death. She liked being an important person in the schools and making the money she did at her business.

In Denver she was never alone. She had many friends to do things with. In Kansas City, she had to learn to do everything alone. Go out to lunch alone, go to a movie alone. This pruning, though it hurt, was necessary for Mary's growth. God pruned Mary down to her real essence with no bells or whistles.

One thing Mary loved to do was go to antique stores and look around. One night she dreamed she was flying on a white horse over a city. Later that day she went to an antique store. There was an old picture on the wall that caught her attention. In the sky, a white horse flew over the city exactly like her dream.

That evening, Dennis and Mary went to an Orion movie. In the beginning credits, a white horse flew right at them. Mary gasped. The third time with a flying white horse in one day. Mary knew it had to be something from the Lord, but what? She would find out later.

Mary worked for the District Attorney's Office in Victim Witness handling sexual assaults and murder cases. She carried a pager.

When someone was raped, night or day she went to the hospital to be with them. She took the collected samples to the crime lab.

She stayed close to the victims comforting them and helping them navigate the system. Mary felt compassion for victims and she was called on to go to homes and make death notification.

Mary called living in Kansas City her dark night of the soul. The next huge blow was Priscilla was diagnosed with terminal cancer. Mary was devastated because she expected they would grow old together.

Mary went with her to Maryland for radiation treatments. Priscilla asked no questions, but Mary could tell by the way the doctors looked at Mary, that her sister was going to die. They were giving Mary a signal, and felt sorry for her.

Priscilla and Mary studied the Bible passage about storing up treasures in Heaven. Priscilla knew she would not be alive for her children's weddings. They were only 15 and 17 years old. Mary promised, "I'll be there."

Priscilla had one rule, "No crying allowed." Mary kept a stiff upper lip then would cry all the way home and for days.

Why would her sister die just when her husband accepted the Lord? Why would this Christian family be torn apart like this? Mary had many questions with no answers.

Priscilla's husband called to say she was gone. Mary did not take it well. The depression came back. She curled up in a fetal position for three days. Her family was leaving earth one by one. Mary was angry at God, but she also knew He was big enough to take it. No sense hiding it from Him. He knows we are but dust. Our strength comes from Him.

One day she was screaming at God, "Why did you let her die? She did not want to die!"

He gently answered, "She did not want to be born either but look what she would have missed out on."

Mary did not want to be born either, but she turned into someone she could never have imagined. Instead of trusting God, she began to worry about who would be next. Demons were ecstatic over Mary's distrust.

Her sister, only 42, was buried at the Air Force Academy where she was married. Her funeral was in the same beautiful Chapel with the stained-glass windows. Mary sobbed and sobbed. Mary also lost her sister's daughter, not to death, but to anger with Mary. She lost her sister's husband who remarried.

She is still close to her sister's son and loves him very much. She will see her sister again, but sometimes she wants to see her now.

Dennis and Mary lived in Kansas City for seven years. Their oldest son married a wonderful Christian girl he met at college. Mary learned a lot from her and is still learning whenever she can. The first time Mary saw her, God gave her a look into her soul. She was beautiful on the outside, but on the inside, even more beautiful. She was the epitome of Psalms 32:2 "Blessed is the person who the Lord imputes no guilt, in whose spirit is no deceit."

Mary had never seen no guilt in a person to this degree! Her spirit flowed like a river straight to God.

Mary's son said, "I got the best one at college, Mom!" He had never dated and decided he would never marry. Then he met her and courted her the way God would want. What a blessing God gave their whole family when she married him!

People had been taken away, but now God added a woman so special. He added their two identical twin sons 7 years later who love GrandMary and Grandpa Dennis very much. They are amazing boys!

One day, Mary heard from the enemy. God pulled the curtain back. As she ate lunch and read a book, she looked up and saw two demons right above her head. They were only two feet tall, dark, and creepy eyes, moving around in fast jerks. They talked to each other in sinister voices about her, not knowing she could see or hear them. The younger one said, "Who is that?"

"Oh, she used to be a threat to us, but we don't have to worry about her anymore. Her name is not important."

The younger one stared straight into Mary's eyes, then turned to the older one and said, "I would not count her out yet!"

Those were the most encouraging words Mary could have heard even though they came out of a demon's mouth. Don't count me out yet! Mary had never doubted God's love for her and she had no intentions of not following Him. She just had not received any instructions. She felt as if she was floundering, Mary was learning something everywhere she went, especially patience.

Maybe God wanted to see what she would do if spiritual things were not happening as they were back in Denver. She did not know. His ways were not her ways. It was a lot easier to work with people who had never heard the gospel, than those who thought they knew what was right but were wrong. Too much pride in themselves to have the right questions. Their questions focused on how to make life easier for themselves, be more prosperous, more compatible with other people, how to "look like a Christian, and act like a Christian." Acting like a Christian does not make you a Christian.

No questions about "What would Christ have me do for Him, even if it makes people hate me or I have to give something up I have worked so hard to attain?" Everyone seemed fairly successful and not in need. But they did not know they are wretched, pitiful, poor, blind and naked like Mary saw them from the cross and told to die for.

Jesus came for the needy like Mary. The sick need the hospital.

One day Dennis called Mary at work. He said, "I just got a call from Detroit offering me a promotion to move. If we do this, my dad will have to live with us. If I don't go, I will never be offered another promotion. I want you to make the decision. Please pray about it and call me back today."

No pressure! Although Mary had learned early in her Christian journey to submit to her husband, Dennis had learned God gave Mary great discernment. He listened to her and made his decisions accordingly. They both submitted to each other. He would never ask Mary to do something he knew she could never do. It was important to him, she make the decision without pushing her either way.

Mary put her head down on her desk. Her gut wrenched. Moving to Detroit with Dennis' dad were two big negatives. He suffered from PTSD, Parkinson's Disease, dementia, and a temper. Plus, he wanted women to know their place—in the kitchen taking care of the men and keeping their mouth shut. That was not Mary. He had become a Christian and was baptized, but his illnesses were taking over. Dennis had been to Detroit many times and always come home with not one good thing to say about it.

"Oh, Lord, what do I do?" She cried out.

The Unseen Voice said, "Could you do it for four years?"

This was only the second time Mary heard anything from Him in Kansas City. Seven long years of silence.

How long was four years? The time someone could get through college or high school. Although it would be hard on her, she thought she could do it. They would take their youngest son with them.

She called Dennis "Okay, I think we should do it."

When Ford wants you, they mean tomorrow. Dennis left for Detroit while Mary quit her job and put the house on the market. When the realtor gave Mary a selling price, Mary upped it by $5,000. It sold for full price.

Together they looked for a house in Detroit. They found the perfect house. Much bigger and more expensive than any house they had owned.

Ford packed them up and unpacked them in Detroit.

Mary walked out on the porch to look at the 100-year-old trees surrounding her house. A fresh, sweet breeze came up and swirled around Mary wrapping her up as her spirit jumped for joy. She knew her dark night of the soul was over.

Two weeks later, Dennis' dad walked up I-270 and was hit by a car. He thought he could get to Home Depot by crossing an eight-lane highway with cars going 80 miles an hour. He fractured his leg in several places, punctured his lung, and had a head injury. Mary had no idea where the hospital was, they took him to. She just thought he was going for a walk around the neighborhood.

She had to call Dennis at work, "I lost your dad. He is in surgery and might not make it. It is all my fault for letting him go for a walk." Mary had tremendous guilt.

He survived and finally came home with health care aids to take care of him while Mary and Dennis worked.

The health care aids stole food from the freezer, ten of Mary's checks, and some jewelry. It was a mess. One did 45 days in jail and had a felony on her record after Mary was done with her.

They found a church almost immediately that was doctrinally sound, with a loving pastor. They made friends.

Sitting on the shelf was over.

MINISTRY IN MO-TOWN

Shortly after Dennis and Mary moved to Detroit, the flu hit Mary hard. She was down for two weeks. She never really recovered, but found a job.

The achiness and fever never left her. Mary went to the doctor. He thought she might have fibromyalgia. But it was an unknown auto-immune disease, a mystery.

Mary could not sleep and was in severe pain. But she pulled herself out of bed every day and made it to work.

This terrible pain continued year, after year, after year.

Dennis and Mary started getting involved in Sunday School. One night, church friends asked them if they would come to downtown Detroit to start an Alcoholics for Christ meeting. They went to a men's six-month lock-down facility for prisoners coming out or going into prison.

The men were required to attend meetings each day. Mary and Dennis taught from an Alcoholics for Christ book.

They had no idea what they were getting into.

These men were the worst of the worst in Detroit--Drug dealers, murderers and thieves, in and out of prison most of their lives.

When Mary introduced herself, she said, "You're probably wondering what we're doing here. I was sitting in my family room out in the suburbs tonight watching television, when our friends called and asked us to come down here. I really did not want to, but Jesus spoke to me and said, 'I want you to go down there and meet some men I really love.'"

She looked each one of them straight in the eyes, hoping they could see the love of Jesus, and that she had no fear.

They sat up straight, unfolded their arms, and were ready to listen.

Mary and Dennis went faithfully every Thursday night for the next four years. If you were hit and miss, these guys would not come back. They could spot a phony a mile away. They were sick of people using them to make points with God. They wanted truth. No problem. Jesus said, "I am the Truth."

Every six months a new group came in. Dennis and Mary started all over again.

Mary said the same thing, looked them in the eyes with the love of Jesus and watch their spiritual weapons tumble. She could hear the clank on the floor like she did when hers fell off.

Mary learned she could preach. These men did not have good listening skills when men talked. Guards yelled, and most had no men in their lives to mentor them in a righteous way.

When Mary spoke, she held their attention. She spoke truth in the Spirit which went right to their hearts. Some of the men told her they loved her. Others called their fathers or mothers for the first time in decades and asked forgiveness. Some would start to weep as they listened. They clearly heard the Word of God. Free from drugs, their minds were healing.

Mary saw these men as God's warriors diverted by the devil into addiction to render them useless. Many of them knew scriptures while some admitted they had been called to the ministry. They were in a battle that would eventually destroy them if they did not return to the God of their youth. Here was another chance. God had not given up on them.

The group grew. Mary reminded them, "You fell into the trap the devil set for you. He wants to destroy you. But we know one thing—you have the same chance we have to follow God. He has a plan but God will not chain you to it. He will not trap you into it like the demons. He will keep sending His love, mercy and grace to touch your hearts."

Homeless men walked through to get a meal and a bed on freezing winter nights. Mary asked all the men to stand up, show respect, and pray earnestly for them. This was their first baby step to serving God.

She said, "An angel is among them, protecting them, look for him."

From the Bible, Mary learned there was nothing written that God did not want her to learn. Her prayer for herself was that she would learn something new about Jesus every day, even up to her last breath. Ever-increasing. Never stopping.

She never would have saved her early church from a false apostle had she not read the Word and listened to The Unseen Voice. She acted on it like a Warrior protecting God's sheep. It was not something she ever wanted to do. It was her promise to get up and follow Christ.

The ridiculously hard stuff! Mary believed God meant what he said.

Early Saturday mornings, Mary joined other church members to pick up children in an old repaired school bus. They took them to the Good News Club. The kids were given clothes, coats, gloves, hats, candy, and the love of Jesus. They played games, taken to parks in the summer and were treated to snow cones.

In August, the children were given back-packs of school supplies. Detroit proper was a very sad place. The spirit of addiction rained destruction. Mary grieved for the people. It was like living on a planet of death. The murdered bodies and the buildings were going down into a grave of decay.

Mary started preaching at a Federal Woman's Prison. This prison was large and housed women who had broken federal laws.

The first time Mary went by herself to the prison, guards made her sign papers. If she was taken hostage she would not be negotiated for in any way. She was on her own. She had to leave everything she had in a locker except her Bible.

Mary learned what a real search involved. They looked between her toes, under her tongue, in her ears, patted her down so hard, even a soda cracker would be found.

Mary asked herself, "Am I willing to be killed to tell them what I know about God's love?" "Yes." No fear of prisoners or death.

They had a prison choir who sounded professional. Mary was told not to allow any prisoner to get up and sing.

Singing was a reward by the Prison Chaplain for being Christian examples to the others.

Mary preached her sermon on how Jesus wanted to have an everlasting, ever-growing relationship with them. What they had done in the past did not matter. What they did from this day forward, the next ten minutes, and ten minutes after that was all that mattered. If they were willing, God would help them.

She spoke a scripture, *Are any of you in trouble? You should pray.* "The prayers from your mouth when you are in grief or trouble are the most powerful prayers there are. God is closest to the broken-hearted."

Mary knew about the broken-hearted. The first 25 years of her life she felt that brokenness. When people in her family started dying and there was no hope for normal relationships, she kept breaking. The women in prison saw Mary's authenticity.

A prisoner was ready to deliver her baby any minute. Mary asked, "Who of you would stand up in your brokenness and pray for this baby?" About 150 women stood up and lifted prayers to the Lord. This was their first baby step.

The first time Mary left the prison, she looked up where the demons had been, "My name is Mary and I'm back! You were right little one. You *do* have to worry about me. If you take one of His, I'll take ten of yours!" Now that is how Warriors fight the enemy!

She watched many women truly come to the Lord and change their whole way of thinking. She started a small group Bible study. "You are in prison because God wanted to save your life," Mary said. "Now He wants to save you for eternity. You can be freer in prison than you ever were out on the streets." They knew it was true.

Detroit was a hard place to live. Mary saw a murder, a shooting at a stop-light right in front of her. A sniper squad was in her front yard hiding behind her trees, trying to talk a man out of a house two doors down from where she lived. He stole a Mustang and was holding a hostage. He released the hostage but shot himself in the bathroom. Her neighborhood was closed off for hours. No one in or out.

Other things, too numerous to mention. They could not save all of the brokenness in the world. Following God was tricky. You could not do what you thought you should do. Only God knew who He was after.

Mary's neighbor was a lesbian. The Unseen Voice said, "I want you to befriend her." Her dog was a big Doberman and Mary's was a new boxer puppy, Glory. They walked their dogs twice a day for two years as Mary showed her the love of Jesus and helped her and her partner in every way she could.

One day she asked Mary, "What do you think about me being a lesbian?"

Mary said, "I love you as a friend. You asked, so I'm going to tell you. We all draw lines where we will not tread. Before I became a Christian, my line was always changing. What was wrong one day became right the next. Where would it stop?

"But when I found a personal relationship with Christ and started reading His Word, I found great relief and comfort in letting the Lord draw my lines for me. That is where I am content to be."

A couple of days later her dog died. The Unseen Voice said, "You are done."

The neighbor moved. God's grace and mercy gave Mary love for her and that love gave Mary the right to tell her truth. She might not have liked what Mary said, but the love helped her hear it. Dennis joined the sea kayak club at Ford, so they took kayak lessons. Mary could not swim and was afraid of water. They started in a swimming pool turning over and releasing themselves from their kayaks to learn how to save themselves. They bought 17-foot sea kayaks, wet suits, Inuit paddles and kayaked almost every weekend in the summer. Mary enjoyed doing something with Dennis that he really wanted to do.

Their goal was to kayak all the Great Lakes and they got in all but one.

Mary believed kayaking was like hiking in the water. There was a whole new perspective. The water had a very soothing effect on your nerves. You did not worry about anything when you were in the water bouncing gently like being in a womb. They kayaked through beautiful water lilies with pairs of swans, and around uninhabited islands.

Mary did have to go to the bathroom on a deserted island. As she pulled off her wetsuit and started to go, a jogger came within touching distance of her. First time ever of taking a chance.

Once they rented a little cabin in Grand Marais. Mary woke up early and went down to Lake Superior to sit in the sand, listen to the waves, and read her Bible. In her reading, she had just got to Isaiah 60. "Arise and shine, for your light has come."

Mary immediately stood up, and at that second, the sun came up over the horizon.

"The glory of the Lord has risen upon you! See darkness covers the earth and thick darkness is over the peoples, but the Lord rises upon you and His glory appears over you. Nations will come to your light, and kings to the brightness of your dawn. Lift up your eyes and look about you. All assemble and come to you. Your sons come from afar, and your daughters are carried on the arm. Then you will look and be radiant, your heart will throb and swell with joy."

Mary felt the warm honey go through her exactly like Mother's Day, 1975. The sun of God covered her with warm sparkling gold as it raised itself into the morning sky over the water. She basked in the presence of His love. She never wanted it to end. Someday it won't.

Because of Dennis' job and Mary's ministering, they were invited to the most lavish weddings they had ever seen. One had four bands and orchestras playing during the reception. Mary thought back to her little sparse wedding that brought her so much joy.

Mary and Dennis loved going to the new Star Movie Theater. One night a news station reporter was there and asked, "What makes your marriage work?" Dennis said into the camera, "Our marriage works because I put Mary first. Jesus Christ taught me that."

A couple weeks later, Mary and Dennis were chosen for a survivor-type show to be shown in segments during the evening newscast. The winning couple would get their house-payment paid for a year.

They had to sleep on the ground in the middle of February on an island. The cold wind in Detroit felt like being stung by needles. Dennis knew how to handle the cold. Mary would only face such conditions with Dennis by her side.

The Station crew came to their house for at-home footage. Mary felt her old competitiveness rising up, which she hated. They went to church that night and Mary fell on her knees to pray. The answer came quick and clear. They were to pick someone else in the competition and do everything they could to help them win. That direction took all the competitiveness out of Mary. She felt great joy, and Dennis immediately agreed.

In the end, they did not care who won. She liked all the couples. Mary had great fun because God told her to give up the opportunity for money.

Mary and Dennis won a few immunities and participated in all the games. But they were happy when the two young married Detroit homicide police officers won their house payments for one year. Mary and Dennis were the oldest married couple, over 40 years. They spent time looking out for the younger ones. On the ride back to the station, everyone thanked Dennis and Mary for their attitude that showed them what grace and love looked like. That was their reward.

One Thanksgiving Mary had a nervous breakdown. She could not stop crying and did not sleep or three days. The doctor said, "I'm going to have Dennis remove his dad from your house. This is too hard on you."

Mary asked, "Is that the best thing for Dennis' Dad?" "Well, no."

"I want him to go when it is best for him, not best for me."

The doctor wanted to put Mary in the psych ward but she refused. She admitted to suicidal thoughts because of the constant excruciating pain. He gave her his personal cell phone number and told her to call him any time day or night.

Mary agreed to take anti-depressants. They worked. Mary's issues were compounded: so much pain, not sleeping, working hard, and never feeling alone in your own house. She was exhausted and missing her oldest son and daughter-in-law.

Dennis' dad's dementia was getting worse. One night he beat on the bed with his cane, yelled and screamed. He would hide his possessions so the Japanese and Germans from World War II would not steal them, then he couldn't find them. He was sure they were stolen in the middle of the night.

Dennis called the doctor because he could not calm him down. The doctor admitted him to the psych ward to check his medications. A few weeks later the head psychiatrist called Dennis and said he could not allow his dad to come back to their house. He was a danger to himself and to Dennis and Mary.

Dennis said, "Mary, I was just thinking that it was exactly four years ago today, Ford called me to come to Detroit."

Mary had never told Dennis about the four years God mentioned. Wow, she did it! It was not easy, especially being in pain every day. The Unseen Voice knew exactly what to tell her to keep her from saying "No, I absolutely will not go to Detroit!"

God is a God of exacts. It was exactly four years from the call and her head on her desk not knowing what to do. She could see that moving to Detroit had nothing to do with Dennis' promotion. It was for the great ministry God wanted them to do, and the grace He wanted to extend to Dennis' dad.

This taught Mary a good lesson on how deep God's grace reaches. He even convinced Mary to keep her father-in-law in her home. It was a victory.

She did what God wanted her to do. He knew it would be hard on her. He knew she would be in terrible pain. He knew Dennis' dad would have an accident and his head wound would make the PTSD and dementia more severe than ever before.

They found a good nursing home and visited him every day. One visit Mary looked around and asked Dennis, "Why doesn't God just take these people home?" Dennis answered wisely, "Because there is something He still wants us to learn."

At work one day, Mary heard from the Unseen Voice, "You are doing many things well, but you are not doing them for Me."

Mary thought she was doing a lot for Him. She went home and told Dennis about it. They decided not to discuss it, but to pray about it for two weeks. The message was clear. Mary was to quit work. She did not know why.

God doesn't show you too far down the road. It is only faith that you would follow Him.

Mary quit, she was diagnosed with breast cancer. The surgery date was set. She was ready no matter what happened.

She had to sign the surgeon could remove both her breasts and some lymph nodes. She was to be in the hospital for three days, and clear her calendar for three summer months for chemo and radiation.

Since Mary's mother, grandmother, grandfather and sister all died young of cancer, Mary thought she could do this and minister to people getting chemo. She was ready.

When Mary woke up in the recovery room, she lifted up her sheet. The surgeon did not remove either breast or any lymph nodes.

When the surgeon came into the recovery room to talk to her, he said, "I opened you up and something told me to stop." The Unseen Voice? "You're released to go home."

"Be in my office in two weeks. I sent the samples to a better diagnostic pathology center. I'll have more information by then. We may have to do this again."

The samples came back cancer-free. The doctor could not believe it. Mary said, "God did it." He said, "Could be, get your annual breast check-up next year and have a great summer."

During the summer Mary traveled to Baltimore Maryland, to learn about Stephen Ministry. This was a ministry that offered a 12-week training to members of the church, to pair them up with people going through difficult situations so they would not have to go through their problem alone. Mary could see how much this would have helped her.

Mary noticed a lot of women Pastors. She found out her church would help her. She started taking classes on-line completing two years of study in six months. Her church hired her as an associate pastor. She was their first woman pastor. On her first day of work, a line formed outside her office of women who did not want to talk to a male pastor.

Dennis taught the 12-week classes and sat in on the support groups where the ministers met once every two weeks. Mary met twice with the care receivers to see if they qualified for a Stephen Minister and made the assignment. By the time they left Detroit, they had trained 56 Stephen Ministers who were actively working with a Care Receiver. Dennis also ran the Good Cents class for people who were in financial debt. Good cents was required for people who asked for handouts. Mary headed up GriefShare, a grief recovery support group for people who lost loved ones and still needed to talk about it. People came from all over the City.

When Dennis turned 52, he asked their financial planner if he could retire early. He had worked his 30 years of service with Ford. He wanted to teach men at Detroit Teen Challenge, a year in-house program for drug addicts and people with life problems.

Their planner ran the numbers 100 different ways and said, "Yes, you can retire. But it would be good for you to get out of Detroit as soon as you can."

They had to wait until their youngest son finished his college education, but Dennis got to teach the letters of Paul at Teen Challenge--the only non-pastor that ever taught the men! Dennis had the gift of teaching and Mary knew his teaching changed her life. Real study was hard. She dug deep to stay on track for the desired message God wanted to give her. She had to literally put herself in His people's shoes, not try to make it all fit her shoes. She wanted to understand the Word for His gain.

In the meantime, they got a call from their oldest son and his wife who said she was pregnant with identical twins.

There were complications.

Mary prayed for her grandbabies, her son and daughter-in-law all the time. The babies stayed in the womb until they were four pounds and healthy as could be. It was one of God's great miracles.

Mary and Dennis drove back and forth to Kansas City ten times that year. Mary wanted to move back, so she could be a grandmother to them, and they would "know" her.

The first time she was asked to preach in the church was on Mother's Day. God always blessed her on the day of The Unseen Power. She prepared her sermon and drove to the church to practice.

It fell flat. She wondered if she was going to make a fool of herself in front of all these people. She was the first woman pastor at this church, and felt responsible to do well.

She asked God, "What's wrong?"

"You don't love these people. If you try to minister to people you don't love, it is spiritual abuse and I will not be there."

He was so right! She loved the prisoners in their need, but she thought her peers, had everything. The next day she laid at the altar and prayed for God's love for these people.

The day she preached, The Unseen Voice said, "Now enjoy it!" And She did! She was not nervous and felt God's pleasure.

Her sermon was based around a young girl who wanted to leave her mother's house and live in the exciting city.

One day she ran away. Her mother was devastated. She prayed and prayed her daughter would be safe and return.

The mother spent all her money in a photograph booth. She took the strips of pictures, cut them up, and wrote on the back, "I love you, come home." Eventually, she had enough money to take a bus to the city.

Her daughter, finding no job, prostituted herself out for money. Ashamed, she could never go home again.

Her mother traveled throughout the city and taped those pictures of herself everywhere. She put them on store windows, telephone poles, mirrors in bathrooms, and doors, until she ran out of pictures.

She left the city and prayed all the way home.

Her daughter was deeply depressed and washing up in a public bathroom. Something caught her eye down at the bottom of the mirror. She crouched down for a better look. Could it be a picture of her mother? She reached down and peeled it off the mirror, turned it over, and read the back, "I love you. Come home."

She realized she had believed a lie. She started walking home. Her mother saw her coming and praised Jesus.

Her mother said to her, "I don't care where you've been or what you've done, I love you." Jesus has left His picture all over this earth. We walk by and don't see it. We want to live in the exciting city. We believe Satan's lies. But Jesus says, "I don't care where you've been or what you've done, I love you. You are mine. Come home."

When Mary finished preaching, the altar started filling up with people who were not living the way God wanted them to. Mary left the stage and sat in a pew so the people could have their time with Jesus.

Mary officiated at many funerals and weddings for people who had no church home. It was something she could do well. She personalized everything. Comfort for the hurting, and for those getting married, how they needed to use their gifts God gave them for others.

Mary's son and daughter-in-law from Kansas City came to Detroit for Mother's Day. They went to the nursing home to visit with Dennis' dad. They had a good visit. Mary's heart broke for him. She began to weep. God had done His work in Mary's heart. The next day on Mother's Day, he died.

He was buried at the military cemetery in Battle Creek, Michigan. *Amazing Grace* played on speakers as they drove to his gravesite. A 21-gun salute was given by men who also served in World War II.

Dennis gave a beautiful eulogy for him. "More men than were buried died during the war. His dad gave his best for his country. He could finally rest." His father would have loved being honored in such a way.

Six months before Mary and Dennis decided to move back to Kansas City, she answered a call from Joe, a regional chaplain in Chicago. "Would you be interested in being a part-time Marketplace Chaplain in Plymouth, Michigan?"

Mary's first question was, "Isn't it illegal?" "No."

She agreed to meet with him. He explained the job to her. She would visit this company once a week to love the workers, show them you cared, and if they asked, answer their questions about faith. She would be their chaplain.

Joe was looking for someone with credentials and also worked for secular companies. These would not be church people.

Mary felt she belonged more with unbelievers than believers. She had experience both with secular companies and training for the ministry. Bingo! Joe came back the next week to train her as the first woman with two men to work for Marketplace Chaplains in Michigan.

Mary started the job and helped people open up for the next step in their faith. She saw herself as a soul doctor, and was good at it. She helped a divorced woman find the courage to fight for the money owed her in the court order. Another woman's mother was dying of cancer and Mary ministered to her. A woman's nephew went deaf and Mary helped get the money together for his operation.

Dennis put their house on the market so they could move back to Kansas City. It worked out perfectly. Six months after they sold their house, the bottom fell out of the automobile industry. Retirement packages like the one Dennis received disappeared. Forty-five houses in their neighborhood were in foreclosure. They would have been stuck. The Unseen Voice moved them out of Detroit at the perfect time.

When they moved back, the grandchildren were three years old. Today they are 17, 6 foot 2, and extremely smart and gifted boys. They know their GrandMary quite well.

When they moved back to Kansas City, Mary talked to the Marketplace Chaplains in Kansas City. One of their chaplains was getting married and leaving the area so they were interested in giving Mary all her assignments. Mary worked for them for 12 years and at the end, she had ministered in 16 businesses even with her pain every day. She also became a Railroad Chaplain of America for Kansas and Missouri. Mary took over a Chinese Church when their pastor suddenly left. She was on the go. She learned as a child, it was best for her to keep moving.

On Tuesdays Mary and Dennis picked up their grandchildren from pre-school. They took them home fixed them dinner and gave them a bath like Mary's grandma did for her in Iowa. The little twins had great conversations with GrandMary while covered in bubbles.

Dennis taught the Chinese congregation English lessons before the church service, and it grew to 50 people. Mary worked hard on her sermons, sometimes using three different English words that meant the same thing so they would understand. She baptized them when they were ready, and blessed their babies. Many were post-docs doing research at KU Med Center and Stowers Institute. They were smart people who wanted to know about Christianity. Mary hoped what she was teaching them touched their hearts and not just their heads.

One family's parents came and the church found out that their great-grandma had been a Christian. She traveled from village to village teaching Christ. The Boxer rebellion stopped her. Now her children and grandchildren were returning to the faith their grandma believed. God had closed a four-generation circle. Mary baptized all of them.

After working with them four years, Mary turned the church over to another church that had a Chinese pastor. She had something else she needed to concentrate on.

ARMIES THEY KNOW NOT OF

Mary's dad lived in Phoenix with his second wife. They made a point of seeing each other once a year. Either Mary and Dennis traveled to Phoenix or Jim and his wife came to wherever Mary and Dennis lived. They kept in touch by phone.

At the end of August, 2010, Jim's second wife died of cancer. Mary made plans for her Dad's move to come live with her.

A call from Adult Social Services told Mary they had received a complaint. A young woman was having too much influence on Mary's dad. They knew her full name and telephone number. This woman was hired through a care agency and worked in his home for three weeks. She did the laundry, cooked, cleaned and shopped for groceries. She had quit the care agency after his wife died, but for some reason was still there.

Mary called her dad. It was the best conversation she ever had with him. She asked him to forgive her. He seemed stunned, but said, "Yes, I forgive you."

"I love you Dad, and I'll see you soon." Mary had her airline tickets to go see him. "I love you, too." It was very seldom Jim said that to Mary.

Later that day, Mary drove to Leavenworth. As she passed the beautiful fall prairie fields of Kansas, the Unseen Voice clearly said, "It is not your fault if your father dies. Forget about your dad's money. It is not yours. You did not earn it. Nothing is yours unless I give it to you."

These words seemed strange because Mary had no thoughts her dad would die or that his money would be taken. The next day Mary started praying in a way she had never prayed before. "Lord, don't let wolves get him!"

Over and over, the same prayer. She could not stop. She decided to call him again, but there was no answer. She knew her dad was dead.

She called Missing Person's at the Phoenix Police Department. They said they would go to his house and look around. Neither he nor his car were there. They had no proof of a crime committed. No body. No crime scene. Nothing except a frantic daughter.

Mary called the Adult Social Services and asked if they would call Missing Persons to tell them about the complaint they received. They agreed. Without their help, a missing person's case never would have opened.

Mary's first reaction was, "I can't do this!" She was still in a lot of physical pain and feverish. She doubted she could take on more emotional pain.

The head detective of Missing Persons called. She explained to Mary they get many calls about people who are not really missing persons. The caller just does not know where they are.

Although this sounded reasonable, Mary knew in her heart her dad had been murdered. She decided to stay in touch with this police woman. She contacted her every time she felt God's nudge.

A few days later there was a message on Mary's answering machine from Debbie, the caregiver. "Your dad went to Las Vegas for three weeks. He'll call you when he gets back." Mary was certain this message was to stop her from flying to Phoenix as she had planned. It worked. She canceled her airline ticket.

Mary's oldest son received a message on his answering machine. "This is Carmen. Your dad and I got married in Las Vegas. We want to work on our relationship and we want you to leave us alone! We'll call you some time after the first of the year."

This person used Mary's dad's phone and called the wrong number. This was another miracle. Mary would have erased the message immediately, but her son took the message and saved it in case it was needed. A year later, the FBI came and picked it up. They discovered who made the call. It was a friend of Debbie's whose name was not Carmen.

Several miracles happened. Mary found out that Jim's next-door neighbor met him at the mailbox. The next-door neighbor's wife had recently died.

Jim said, "You should talk to Debbie, my caregiver. She is handling everything for me. She's is my angel!" Debbie came out of the house and hurried Jim away from his neighbor. From that time on, she got all the mail.

The next-door neighbor thought she had too much influence on Jim, so he called his daughter who was an attorney. Attorneys are mandatory reporters of suspected abuse to the proper agency. She called Adult Protective Services in Phoenix.

When Adult Protective Services went to check on Jim, Debbie told them she was her mother's name instead of her own. The investigators knew Debbie's mother who had been involved in other claims of elder abuse. Debbie then gave them her real name, cell phone number and the attorney's number she had used to change Jim's will to make her executor of his estate. She told them Jim wanted this and he was of sound mind. Mary's dad agreed. Mary was still the only beneficiary.

God was setting Debbie up to get caught.

The Missing Persons Detective called Mary. Debbie said Jim left town in a red convertible with a woman named Carmen. He had all his money with him and Debbie was finished taking care of him. As far as they were concerned the case could close. More wolf-devil lies from Debbie.

Mary's only hope was to keep calling Missing Persons, but she had to have a reason. She knew not to pester the police or sound like a nut case. She decided to come up with small assignments for them so they would not close the case.

At various times, Mary called, "Could you ask Debbie if she has heard from my dad?" "Tell her if she has my dad call me just once I will not bother him again."

"What if this was your father, would you want the case closed?"

"I know my dad is dead, I'm doing this to save the next elderly person she is going to kill." Nothing worked to find Jim, but the case stayed open.

Her calls kept her relationship growing with the Detective. Mary and Debbie were in a sword fight for the ear and trust of the Missing Person's Detective. Mary felt sooner or later truth would prevail. God is truth and the most powerful force in the universe.

Debbie told the detective that Mary and her dad were not close. Mary did not even come to her step-mother's funeral.

When the detective relayed that information, Mary said, "I don't know why Debbie would say that. She was there during that time. I offered to come and officiate the funeral, but they cremated her so quickly, there was no funeral. Call my dad's step-children and ask them."

The detective did and caught Debbie in her first lie. It wasn't much, but it was a start.

The last time Mary talked to her dad was September 9, 2010. She knew he was dead the next day. She also knew the longer this charade dragged on, the less chance there would be of catching Debbie or finding her dad's body. As each day passed, Mary was more disheartened. Nevertheless, she persisted.

Mary started having panic attacks in the daytime and nightmares at night. She saw his flesh eaten and bones chewed on by desert animals. He called Mary's name to help him and she could not get to him. Several times at a grocery store, Mary had to be escorted to her car because she was frozen and could not move or breathe. Other times she called Dennis. He talked her through check-out and helped her get home. She could not be around many people.

Throughout this tragedy and pain, Mary was not mad at God. It wasn't God's doing, but the devil's plot. Mary knew God had chosen her as the daughter-Warrior who would stop this serial killer. She knew God was with her dad during every second of his demise.

Mary's pain and depression worsened but nothing could be done. She just kept *"Getting up and following Him."*

On one of her calls to her new-found friend, the Missing Person's Detective, the Detective said Debbie told her Jim and Carmen went to Mexico. Mary knew her dad would never go to Mexico. He was afraid of all the drug wars on the border. He kept himself safe in a secure community on a golf course.

The Detective said they put pictures of Jim on all border crossings in case he crossed from the USA to Mexico or from Mexico to the USA. He would be picked up by Border Patrol. Now ICE was involved.

Mary said "Thanks," but knew he was dead.

A lady from one of Mary's Bible studies said, "Remember, you have armies they know not of." Mary hung onto those words and thanked her later for sharing that truth.

The woman said, "I never said that!" "That is something I would never say." "Yes, you did, I heard you clearly."

The Unseen Voice used someone else to say His words.

Mary had an army of Angels who would not be defeated, working behind the scenes on what she could not do; in places she could not go. God wanted her to know it. She had been completely overwhelmed thinking this was all up to her. Her part was minor—keep calling the Detective and give her small things to do.

God does not always take grief and pain away. He gives help to endure it and be victorious. That one sentence about the armies gave Mary a glimmer of hope, confidence and fight. Anyone who did not believe her did not matter. She still had a Heavenly army fighting harder to stop Debbie than she was. Mary was not alone!

She knew in her soul God wanted her stopped before she killed again. Debbie murdered Mary's father, sold his house and kept the money, and took everything he had, to crawled into Mary's life and brought her into the battle. Every call Mary made was an arrow going Debbie's direction. Mary had to learn those calls were her only assignment.

One afternoon a man called. He tried to sound elderly. "Mary?"

"Yes."

"Ah, sweetie pie and I are traveling and having a good time. I do not want to come live with you in Kansas City." Click.

Were these people stupid? Did they think Mary would not know her own father's voice? This was Debbie's answer to Mary's call to the Detective, "Tell Debbie to have him call me once and I will never bother him again."

Mary immediately went into a full-fledged panic attack because it was not her dad. However, Jim called her mom sweetie and his second wife sweetie, so this person had some personal knowledge of him.

Right in the middle of a huge panic attack and unable to breathe, Mary dialed the Homicide Detective's number. He picked right up. She talked to him through trying to breathe and gave him the number that showed up on her phone. It was a Houston, Texas, prefix. He put the Missing Person Detective on the phone to try to calm Mary down.

The Homicide Detective checked with the telephone company and found out the ping had just come from a cell tower by Debbie's house.

The police wanted Mary to call the number back and ask for her dad. When she did, the phone was dead. It was a kill phone used for one call only. Mary knew only criminals used kill phones. If Mary knew that fact, the Phoenix police would know it, too.

As excruciatingly painful as this was to Mary, it was the best thing that could have happened. It broke the case open. With this new information, the deputy district attorney was able to get a warrant to search the house Debbie and her mother lived in on their 10-acre property. Cadaver dogs and helicopters were combing every inch. No Jim.

They did find paperwork that Debbie had done this to another man shortly before Jim. She had taken $200,000 from him and cashed in his life insurance check. She had taken him to her notary with her doctor saying he was of sound mind. He had brain cancer and had no idea what was happening.

Another miracle. Mary was home to answer that phone call. The caller sounded surprised when she picked up. If he had left a voice mail and Mary would have heard it a couple of hours later, it would have taken months to trace where the kill phone pinged.

In the middle of all this, Mary went to a weekend retreat in Excelsior Springs, Missouri. It was a beautiful refurbished hotel where Truman stayed when he won the Presidency. Mary thought it might be good for her to get away for a few days and focus on something else.

As part of the retreat, everyone was given a laminated scripture that had been prayed over. In a room of 150 women, Mary's scripture said: "Then you will find your joy in the Lord and I will cause you to ride on the heights of the land, and to feast on the inheritance of your father. The mouth of the Lord has spoken." (Isaiah 58:14)

Mary focused on riding on the heights of the land (on a white horse maybe?) and finding joy. Joy had been missing from Mary for quite some time. The Lord said it was coming.

The Missing Person Detective called Mary to tell her she caught Debbie in another lie. Debbie made the mistake of telling the Detective that she did know where Jim was and was sending him money.

The Detective said, "You told me you did not know where he was and he had all his money. Give me his address."

Debbie went into her bedroom and came out with a little piece of paper with a handwritten address on it of a little town in Mexico. The Detective called the American Embassy Consulate Police to check it out. Nobody was there by that name. No one had ever lived there by that name. No mail had ever been received to that name.

Debbie was breaking down under the pressure. The Unseen Voice spoke to the Detective "Go check the bank accounts."

The Detective went to the bank and discovered Debbie had all of Jim's money and was using it for herself. How could he travel to Mexico with no money? Debbie was still cashing Jim's retirement checks and filling his deceased wife's prescriptions for morphine.

About a month later, the Phoenix Missing Persons called and told Mary, "We hate to tell you this, but we believe your dad is dead."

Mary said, "I know he's dead!"

They expected her to cry, but she was so relieved that finally, somebody actually believed her! It was still an open investigation and they could not tell her anything except they still had not found her father's body.

Mary knew a lot was going on behind the scenes now that they believed Jim had been murdered. Time drug on without hearing a word.

Then one day as Mary was about to leave one of her chaplain clients, a policeman from Phoenix called. "We arrested Debbie and her son today at the airport. They were getting on a plane going to Europe. She has all your dad's money including what she sold his house for, and we found your dad's car repainted in her son's high school parking lot. We wanted you to know before it goes on the news tonight or hits the papers. That's all we can tell you."

Mary's oldest son called her after he received the same call from the police and said, "Good job, Mom."

Mary almost dropped to the floor with relief. Debbie did not get away with it. Mary heard later that Debbie got sick when they arrested her. They had to drag her out of the airport. Her son was also arrested for grand theft auto and forging the Title to Jim's car with Photoshop that Debbie purchased with Mary's step-mother's credit card.

Mary wondered if Debbie's destination in Europe was a country that had no extradition treaty with the United States to send her back.

God was teaching Mary patience and trust. Mary wanted to be there working the case with the police, but that could not happen.

During this time of great stress, Mary suffered excruciating pain and panic attacks. But she was encouraged by several reminders about the white horse and "riding on the heights of the land," and the three flying white horses she saw in one day so many years ago. She knew a white horse was waiting for her in God's stables. She would ride with Him and be His Warrior while Jesus handed out justice.

Sometimes her white horse showed up at her bedside. He crouched by her bed and she rolled onto him. He took her for a ride.

Sometimes he showed up in the middle of the day--long rides, short rides. They always brought her joy. She hung onto his thick white main. No stirrups, no reins, ropes, or saddle on this horse. Her legs did not fit well around his large girth. She laid on him with her legs going backwards instead of straight down.

If she thought about going a certain way, he gently turned. Nothing physical was necessary. If he felt her getting out of balance, he adjusted himself perfectly. He whinnied when he was ready for a ride. His hooves hardly touched the ground, so there was no clip-clop. His wings made a relaxing whooshing sound, and Mary's view on his back was perfect.

She could see other countries. One night they went to the pyramids and he got Mary close enough to touch them.

When she woke up the next morning, the pyramids were on the TV news.

He came and left at someone else's command. But it was always a relief. This beautiful horse helped her through one of the hardest times of her life. This magnificent mount relieved her of pain and sorrow, if even for a little while!

One night her stallion stood next to Mary's bed. She and the white horse heard someone whistle. They both looked in the same direction.

The Unseen Voice called, "Justice!"

The horse turned on his hooves and went to his Master. Justice was his name. Mary did not have to wait until she got to Heaven to find out his name! God is the God of love, mercy and justice. Mary was seeking justice for her dad and who knows how many other people who were killed and robbed before Jim or would have been after Jim? She was already trolling the internet for her next victim looking for rich men who had no family in Phoenix.

Justice still came to take her riding like her friends would let her ride their horses years ago when she was aching in her soul because she was invisible to her family. Dennis would come in his dad's jeep to take her explore God's beauty in the Rocky Mountains and plan their future. Kayaks would skim on the Great Lakes between the water lilies with the swans and water cupping around her. God always gave Mary a respite when she endured some very hard experiences! Christ always let her escape for a while and truly enjoy the horses, the jeep, the kayaks and her heavenly horse!

It took two years to arrest Debbie and five years for the trial to begin. When Mary got on the stand to testify, Debbie stared at Mary and Mary stared back. Mary's thoughts were saying, *"I am here. I know who you are and what you are."* Debbie's defeated head dropped. She never looked up at Mary again. God's Warriors never cower to the enemy of this world.

The Deputy District Attorney (DDA) was amazing and had moved to Phoenix to work on Jim's case. He only worked on cases where no bodies were found. He sliced the case up with the skill of a surgeon and presented it in such a way all of Debbie's appeals were denied. The DDA had it pinned down to the very 15 minutes on the day Mary was praying, "Don't let the wolves get him." The wolves didn't get him, the Shepherd did.

God, Mary and Debbie were the only ones who knew the truth. Mary could not give up. The Unseen Power had trained her everywhere she went and chose her for this capture. Debbie was proven diabolical and sentenced to life in prison without the possibility of parole. Mary's father had no chance. The world is a little safer. Mary would never have to see her again or go to a parole hearing.

God worked his many miracles. Mary made her calls; Armies they know not of guided the police and investigators to the right places to solve a mystery in Satan's well-hidden dark holes.

The trial took three months. Mary and Dennis went back and forth to Phoenix about eight times, but could not stay for the whole trial. There are things Mary does not know since they did not hear all of it. Mary was still having panic attacks and in horrible pain. At one point, Justice quit coming. Mary took it as a good sign that Jesus knew she was getting better and would not need him. He will be waiting to ride and nuzzle.

In Mary's Victim Impact Statement, she read to the Judge and Debbie, "I forgive Debbie, Jesus Christ taught me that. You can be redeemed, even in prison." It took Mary five long years to be able to say that and mean it. Like grief, true forgiveness is a process.

Debbie picked on a father who had a Warrior for a daughter and Armies they knew not of. To this day they have never found Jim's body. God knowing is good enough for Mary. Jim's inheritance he left to Mary was all turned over to her exactly like it would have been if he had died of natural causes on the day he was murdered.

Mary kept the promises she wrote to herself, The Unseen Power, and Unseen Voice as a child, a young woman, and a grandmother with the help of God. She is looking forward to seeing Him face-to-face, eat from the Tree of Life, and ride Justice forever waiting for her.

Even though Mary was going through grief with her father, her assignments from God did not stop, in fact, they picked up.

She helped family members of railroad deaths and severe trauma. One young man had laid down on the tracks and was drug by the train. He survived to go to his high school prom and graduation.

When couples considered divorce, Mary pulled them back to their first love for each other. When people wanted to commit suicide, were depressed, or just lost in a broken world, Mary reminded them the demons are never as strong as God's power. Mary helped them see God's light in every situation and showed them how to find the truth instead of living in fear, shame and false guilt. She was the Warrior God used to speak His Truth.

Mary led people to the Lord of their youth right before they died. One woman was 100 years old. Another one wanted to go and when Mary sang songs to her, she remembered them from her youth in Sunday School and sang along. All things became new for her.

She prayed for four people the doctors said would die but God healed them immediately. Only God knows who the next one will be.

She officiated many funerals for people in motorcycle gangs, the Mafia, and on the back of a trailer porch while people smoked and drank their beers.

She performed many marriages having the couples realize what marriage vows really mean.

She stopped a legion of strong demons from Haiti in their tracks after the KU psych ward head psychiatrist said they couldn't help a young woman's torment from a curse every few minutes trying to pull her into hell. The psychiatrist said she should find a church. The demons were stronger than their medicine. She miraculously drove right into Mary's church parking lot as Mary pulled in. She was released from the demons as Mary prayed the Holy Spirit be sent to Haiti and the light of the Lord pull her uncle, a witch-doctor in charge of a large demonic group, into God's love.

When the young woman returned to Haiti, her whole family had stopped witchcraft and were serving the Lord.

The demons knew Mary's name.

Mary ministered to addicted people and God snuffed out their addictions.

God was showing Mary that even though she was going through grief and pain of her own, He was her Commander in Chief and if she "Got up and Followed Him," miracles would happen. They did. She did whatever He asked her to do with no hesitation.

For the first 25 years of Mary's life, all she wanted to do was get away from her family. But in the end, she was the one who stayed and took care of them as they left this earth. Just as she saw a new day dawning for them, they died. It was so hard watching them go.

She came to realize their new day dawned. God turned off their living room light as the eternal sun came up.

She gave her mom baths, took her to the bathroom, and wiped the blood off her face when she had coughing fits from lung cancer. She went and stayed with her sister when she had radiation, and visited her many times caring for her and her children during cancer treatments. She was at both Priscilla's children's weddings. She reminding her brother to honor his father and if he did not forgive, Christ would not forgive him. She stayed on task with the Phoenix Police Department to stop the serial killer who murdered her father.

Mary could not make anything happen. She could only be obedient to the lover of her soul.

It is still baby steps. Mary often thinks about what life would have been like if The Unseen Power had not put her on the floor on Mother's Day 1975--a wasted life of self-pity.

These 44 years have been like finding a precious jewel every day. Mary believes she knows God differently than most people because He has graciously illuminated Himself to her. He pulled the curtain back over and over to show her Truth.

Mary's life changed from being invisible and unloved, to following Jesus and knowing her purpose. She has never been invisible to the one true God.

Mary kept her promise to "Get up and Follow Me." She kept her promise when she stood before God with her wedding Bible in her hand. Mary and Dennis have been faithful and true to each other, and in 2019, they will celebrate their 50th anniversary.

She kept her promise to forgive her Mother and Father and honor them the rest of her life. She kept her promise to love her children and grandchildren uncondithionally.

She kept her promise to forgive all those who hurt her, realizing we do not fight against flesh and blood, but against principalities and powers in dark places.

She kept her promise to keep Dennis' dad for four years and take care of him the best she could. She kept her promise to honor her dad's wishes to keep the inheritance he wanted her to have.

Through all the heartache Mary endured, she straightened her feeble knees and stood up. She learned to *"let go"* of what God peeled from her hands.

Satan tried to kill her more times than she will ever know, but The Unseen Voice always intervened. Best of all, she knows she is His favorite (or one of them).

Mary is not expecting the rest of her life to be like standing on pillows. She expects to be walking on sharp rocks, taking bruises, hits that cut like a boxer until Christ calls her name and takes her to the home He has prepared for her for other warrior assignments.

That little girl laying in her bed crying because nobody loved her did not fit into her family or this world. But The Unseen Voice said, "Don't let them define who you are, you are my visible Warrior to be reckoned with!"

The Unseen Voice said, "I want you to write a book."

EPILOGUE

1. Realize that God can change you in the twinkling of an eye no matter what you've done. He is the Master heart changer.

2. Read your Bible. Don't use a spoon on the surface like young Mary did trying to dig to China, but a pick-ax to pull out the real jewels. Spend time thinking about why God is using the words He is. Who is He talking to? What does it say to you? Write it down somewhere and meditate on it. He loves nothing more than someone interested in His Word. Read his *whole* Bible to get a realistic picture of Him and what is Truth. Stand up. Straighten your feeble knees. Throw excuses into the sea. You are not too busy, and the devil's lies will all be debunked. Take His Word by the horns as if your life depended on it. It does.

3. Know who is in you and what mighty strength and power He has. Never fear anyone or any demon. They get stronger by your fear. God is your protector and you have armies they know not of.

4. Step out with the first, second, and third baby steps. Never stop. It will become easier each time, but your life will actually be harder. If He asks, He will help you do it.

5. Realize that there is a world swirling around all of us in the spiritual realm. Know it exists. He will hold the curtain back to give you a peek. Open your eyes to see and your ears to hear.

6. Spend your life perfecting your love for God and for all people. Love will draw them to Him. Don't expect anything in return. You may get hate, but those are still the people He died for.

7. Hold whatever you've attained loosely. He may transplant you and prune you for the purpose He created you for. This is not a failure, it is a step up. Look forward to a city with foundations, whose architect and builder is God. That is our true eternal reward.

8. Rejoice that someday the curse we live under will be gone, and death, pain and tears will be no more.

"Justice will role like a river, righteousness like a never-failing stream" Amos 5:25

Made in the USA
Monee, IL
16 June 2021

71512454R00074